Three Acts of Love

The Start of Space by Laura Lindow

fangirl, or the justification of limerence by Naomi Obeng

with the love of neither god nor state by Vici Wreford-Sinnott

T0179858

methuen | drama

LONDON • NEW YORK • OXFORD • NEW DELHI • SYDNEY

METHUEN DRAMA
Bloomsbury Publishing Plc
50 Bedford Square, London, WC1B 3DP, UK
1385 Broadway, New York, NY 10018, USA
29 Earlsfort Terrace, Dublin 2, Ireland

BLOOMSBURY, METHUEN DRAMA and the Methuen
Drama logo are trademarks of Bloomsbury Publishing Plc

First published in Great Britain 2023

Design by Ignatz Johnson Higham & Ana Stefaniak

A catalogue record for this book is available from the British Library.

A catalog record for this book is available from the Library of Congress.

ISBN: PB: 978-1-3504-5461-3
ePDF: 978-1-3504-5462-0
eBook: 978-1-3504-5463-7

Series: Modern Plays

Typeset by Mark Heslington Ltd, Scarborough, North Yorkshire

To find out more about our authors and books visit
www.bloomsbury.com and sign up for our newsletters.

Laura Lindow, Naomi Obeng & Vici Wreford-Sinnott

A Live Theatre production

Three Acts of Love

Passion. Obsession. Acceptance. Betrayal.

Thursday 30 November – Saturday 16 December 2023

Three Acts of Love

By **Laura Lindow, Naomi Obeng & Vici Wreford-Sinnott**

CAST

Imogen Stubbs

Rebecca Glendenning-Laycock

Laila Zaidi

CREATIVE & PRODUCTION TEAM

Laura Lindow	Writer
Naomi Obeng	Writer
Vici Wreford-Sinnott	Writer
Me Lost Me	Score, Live Music & Sound
Jack McNamara	Co-Director
Bex Bowsher	Co-Director
Amy Watts	Set & Costume Designer
Drummond Orr	Lighting Designer & Production Manager
Alicia Meehan	Movement
David Flynn	Associate Sound Designer
Virginia Mayes-Wright	Stage Manager
Kamilla Jonsson	Deputy Stage Manager
Taylor Howie	Technician

Passion. Obsession. Acceptance. Betrayal.

Three Acts of Love brings together three stories each exploring what love means in the world today. From a closing social club to internet fandom via an animated lecture by a heart-broken heart surgeon, the play takes the audience on an incredible journey through this most complex and crucial emotion.

A young runaway finds unexpected shelter in a local social club from a world that doesn't understand her.

A surgeon who lectures on matters of the heart confesses a dark and unexpected truth of her own.

An obsessive fan will do anything to protect her idol's reputation, including posing as him online.

Foreword

'Heartbreak is at the heart of all revolutionary consciousness. How can it not be? Who can imagine another world unless they already have been broken apart by the world we are in?'

– Gargi Bhattacharyya

We started with a simple premise. For three playwrights to offer their responses to the word love in the final production for Live Theatre's 50th anniversary season. The key was in selecting writers so radical in their thinking that even such an overused word would receive a new lease of life.

We were not even a year out of lockdown when this project was conceived. Love was in the air but so were a lot of things; fear, confusion, longing, maybe even a touch of hate. In launching a project about 'love' at this time we knew it wasn't likely to contain any dating or marriage stories. Love had come to mean something more complex altogether. These three writers would ensure that.

Vici Wreford-Sinnott was clear from the start of what her approach would be. A deeply political thinker she went straight for the jugular in setting her piece *with the love of neither god nor state* in a social club. In the North East in particular such a space has a very particular meaning. A place of warmth and togetherness for many. But not everyone. Like Greta the runaway with an invisible disability. This is not traditionally a space associated with such a person, yet Vici turns tradition on its head making the club somewhere a disabled woman might actually call home.

Laura Lindow is a multi-talent to say the least; writer, director, producer, educator and clown doctor known to some as Doctor Lulu McDoo, working with hospitalised children and their families mainly in the cardiothoracic unit. Her piece goes directly and quite literally to the heart. Her story *The Start of Space* is told by a female heart surgeon (one of only a very few in the country) who gives a lecture to future doctors and in doing so reveals a hidden heartbreak of her own. The love Laura brings and feels for this lifesaving key worker goes far beyond a round of applause in a doorway.

A unique and almost musical thinker, Naomi Obeng's response to love was to dive into its darker recesses; obsession, attachment, detachment, desire. Her terrain is the scorched landscape of internet fandom where the lines between the real and the projected, the felt and the imagined blurred into a single stream of experience. Her piece *fangirl* never writes off the emptiness of the digital realm but instead makes a church of it; a space of communion that ignites hopes and desires for better and definitely for worse.

The fourth voice who doesn't make it into these pages is the musician live onstage. In our case this is Jayne Dent AKA Me Lost Me, a singular artist as at home with ancient folk as she is with the deep pulse of electronics. Her sounds and her voice merge like a river flowing through and past each of these brief snapshots of love. A love that can be hard to see, shrouded as it is in so many painful things, but now more needed than ever.

Jack McNamara
Artistic Director of Live Theatre, November 2023

Cast

Imogen Stubbs

Imogen was born in Rothbury Cottage Hospital. She lived briefly in Portsmouth, where her father was a naval officer, before moving to London where she grew up on an old Thames sailing barge.

She spent pretty much every childhood holiday at her grandmother's house between Cambo and Rothbury – in a magical place called Rothley.

Her extensive TV credits include: D H Lawrence's *The Rainbow*; the BBC's very silly *Big Kids*; *Anna Lee*; Terence Rattigan's *The Browning Version* and *After the Dance*; Alan Ayckbourne's *Relatively Speaking* and a role in the final series of Netflix's *The Crown*.

Her many credits in the West End and varied wonderful regional theatres include: *A Streetcar Named Desire*; *St Joan*; *Closer*; *Uncle Vanya*; *Heartbreak House*; *Three Sisters*; *The Glass Menagerie*; *Orpheus Descending*; *Private Lives*; *Mum's the Word*; *The Boyfriend*; *A Marvellous Year for Plums*; *The Hypochondriac*; *A Blast from the Past*.

Recent stage credits include: *Clybourne Park* (Park Theatre); *Honour* (Park Theatre); *The Be All and End All* (York Theatre Royal); *Things I Know To Be True* (Frantic Assembly – The Lyric); *Communicating Doors* (Menier Chocolate Factory); *Elephants* (Hampstead Theatre); *Alecky Blythe's Little Revolution* (Almeida Theatre); *Strangers on a Train* (The Gielgud); *The Children* (Theatre Royal, Bury St Edmunds); *Salt, Root and Roe* (The Donmar); *Third Finger Left Hand* (Trafalgar Studios).

Rebecca Glendenning-Laycock

Rebecca is an actor, writer and theatre maker based in Newcastle upon Tyne. As a maker Rebecca's work is funny and refreshing with a tender middle. As a performer Rebecca has most recently worked with The Customs House, Live Theatre, Alphabetti Theatre and Curious Monkey. Rebecca was also a founding member of queer theatre company Bonnie and The Bonnettes, and made shows with them from 2016 until their close in 2022. These shows included *Drag Me to Love; And She; Bonnie and Fanny's Christmas Spectacular.*

For the Royal Shakespeare Company, she appeared in *Othello*, *Two Noble Kinsmen*, *The Rover* and *Richard II*. For the National she appeared in *The Relapse* and *Betrayal*.

Film credits include: *Jack & Sarah*, *Twelfth Night*, *True Colors*, *Fellow Traveller*, *Deadline*, *A Summer Story*, *Erik the Viking* and *Sense and Sensibility*.

Laila Zaidi

Theatre credits include: Clem – *Little Bits of Light* (National Theatre); Maria – *West Side Story* (Kilworth House and RSC); Charlie – *The Selfish Giant* (Vaudeville Theatre); Tassita – *Starlight Express* (The Other Palace Theatre); Jess – *Bend It Like Beckham* (Toronto); Polly – *The Boyfriend* (Menier Chocolate Factory); Sashi – *Invisible* (Bush Theatre); Clare – *The Season Ticket* (Northern Stage); Frankie – *Frankie Goes To Bollywood* (Rifco Theatre).

TV credits include: *Ackley Bridge* S5 (Channel 4); *Benidorm* S10 (ITV); *Mood* (BBC); *Doctors* (BBC); *Dog Days* (Comedy Pilot); *Holby City* (BBC).

Short films include: *The Everlasting Club* (Jeva Films Productions); *Hayley Allen* (Rebel Park Productions).

Voiceover credits include: BBC Radio Summer of Sport; BBC Sounds – Young Writers Awards Shortlist narration; Audiobook *The Nutcracker* by Alex T Smith (Audible); Sky Radio Christmas advert.

Laura Lindow

Writer – The Start of Space

Laura is a Scottish writer and director who has proudly lived and worked in the North East for over twenty years.

Writing credits include: Act 3 to Julia Darling's *Manifesto for a New City* for Newcastle's Theatre Royal; *Baba Yaga* for Theatre Hullabaloo; *The Sorcerer's Apprentice*, *The Emperor's New Clothes*, *The Snow Queen* and HG Wells' *The War of the Worlds* adapted for Northern Stage; *The Christmas Tree* for Durham's Gala; *The Ultimate Pickle* for Paines Plough (Roundabout 2022); *Pause* for Alphabetti Theatre; *The Important Man*, *Credit* and *Woven Bones* for Cap-a-Pie; *Beyond the End of the Road* for November Club; *Heartbreak Soup* for Laura Lindow/The Empty Space; and *Tidal*, Novak's immersive instillation at the Laing Art Gallery as part of the Lindisfarne Gospel's exhibition, 2022.

Directing credits include: Open Clasp's *Key Change* (winner of Carol Tambor 'Best of Edinburgh Award' 2015 with New York Transfer, Critics Pick in *The New York Times* and Winner of Best Overall Event Journal Culture Awards 2017); *Don't Forget the Birds* (Journal Culture Awards' Performance of the Year 2019); *Sugar* (broadcast 2019/20 on BBC iPlayer); *Lasagna (the film)* & *Lasagna (Live Tour)* 2023; *Mycelial* (theatre for film, currently in edit for cinema broadcast in 2024). All the above as Associate Director for Open Clasp Theatre Company 2014–23. Additionally *Donna Disco* for Chicken Pox Fox and *Preggers* for Curious Monkey.

Laura regularly facilitates, mentors and dramaturgically supports writers, writing groups and creative projects both regionally and nationally, including recently supporting parents and carers writing for York University's recent publication *A Year Like No Other – Life on a Low Income during Covid 19*, giving first-hand accounts of surviving on a low income throughout the pandemic and urgently arguing for systemic change.

She was part of The Royal Court Writers' Group (North) in 2018/2019, and received a Journal Culture Award in 2019 for 'Writer of the Year'.

A Clown Doctor of 16 years for Tin Arts, she treads the wards as Dr Lulu McDoo, working with hospitalised children and their families. In addition, Laura is delighted to be New Writing North & Newcastle Hospitals Charity's recently appointed *Writer in Residence*.

Naomi Obeng

Writer – fangirl

Naomi Obeng is an artist and playwright interested in creating new worlds on stage that help us to better understand our own. She embraces the strange and the absurd in order to twist familiar thought processes, upset social apathy and ask difficult questions about our contemporary status quo.

Her recent work includes: *We'll Be Who We Are*, her first full-length play which was shortlisted for the Women's Prize for Playwriting (2020) and previewed at VAULT Festival (2023); *Where it Lands* for Nottingham Playhouse; *New Town Cry* for New Perspectives; *A Distance Between* for Paines Plough's 'Come To Where I'm From'.

She has developed work as part of NO BORDERS at the Royal Court and English Touring Theatre's Nationwide Voices. She has been supported as a playwright by Soho Writers Lab, Royal Court Introduction to Playwriting Group, Leicester Curve as a resident writer, and New Perspectives as a New Associate.

Vici Wreford Sinnott

Writer – with the love of neither god nor state

Vici is a writer/director for theatre, screen and radio from the North East where she founded Little Cog, a disabled-led theatre company, in 2011. Vici is a leading figure in the UK Disability Arts Movement, a proud Associate Artist at ARC Stockton and is thrilled to have been awarded a studentship for her own practice-based PhD research into Radical Acts: Disabled Women Performing from Teesside University. Vici is under commission to Live Theatre for a full production of her play *Useless F*cker* and is currently developing her one woman show *Wrapping Myself in All the Women I Could Have Been* for a national tour. In 2021 Vici was awarded the Journal Arts and Culture Award for Outstanding Contribution to the arts in the region.

Vici's original theatre work includes: *Butterfly* (Best One Person Play 2018 British Theatre Guide, national tour); *Lighthouse* (bilingual piece in English and BSL, British Premiere ARC Stockton); *Another England* (national tour); *The Art of Not Getting Lost* (ARC Stockton and Northern Stage); *Vote for Caliban* (Northern Stage); *Deadly Devotchka* (Edinburgh Fringe); *Moll Cutpurse: A Comedy for the 21st Century* (UK and Ireland tour). Vici has many directing credits and has mentored many disabled writers to bring their work to the stage.

Vici was commissioned by the BBC to write and direct her short film *Hen Night* creating one of the first ever pieces of broadcast British drama by a disabled women-led team. Films include *Funny Peculiar* starring BBC Silent Witness actor Liz Carr for Northern Stage and ARC Stockton; *Siege* was commissioned by Home Manchester and ARC Stockton Homemakers with her accompanying non-fiction series *The Wrong Woman Discussions* featuring four other disabled women performing in the public eye. Vici's radio drama *The UnSung* was commissioned by Durham Book Festival, New Writing North and ARC Stockton.

Jack McNamara

Co-Director

Jack has been Artistic Director and Joint CEO of Live Theatre in Newcastle since 2021. Productions for the company as director include: *The Cold Buffet*; *We Are The Best!*; *One Off*. Previously he was Artistic Director of New Perspectives in Nottingham, where productions included the multiple award-winning *The Fishermen* (West End, Home Manchester, BBC Radio 3, British Council Showcase); *The Lovesong of Alfred J Hitchcock* (Off Broadway); *The Boss of It All* (Soho Theatre/Offie nominated); *Darkness Darkness* (Nottingham Playhouse) and first national tours of plays by Athol Fugard and debbie tucker green among many others. Recent freelance work includes *Shy* by Max Porter (Southbank Centre) starring Toby Jones and Ruth Wilson. He directed the epic audiobook *Voice of the Fire* by Alan Moore starring Maxine Peake, Mark Gatiss and Jason Williamson of Sleaford Mods.

Bex Bowsher

Co-Director

Bex is dedicated to developing new voices and has worked with Graeae, BBC Writer's Room and theatre companies across the UK. She is the Chair of the Board of Unfolding Theatre, and is a playwright alongside her directing practice. Bex is dedicated to creating work that creates space for those who are typically othered by society. Theatre credits include: *Love It If We Beat Them and One Off* (Live Theatre); *Sorcerer's Apprentice* (Northern Stage).

Amy Watts

Set & Costume Designer

Amy graduated from Wimbledon College of Art with a BA (Hons) in Theatre Design. Her credits include: Associate Designer: *Wet House* (Live Theatre). Assistant Designer: *Othello* (ENO). Designer: *The Bat With No Bite* (Northern Stage); *Much Ado About Nothing* (Creation Theatre); *Hedda Gabler* (Reading Rep); *Jack, Mum and the Beanstalk* (Hull Truck); *The Massive Tragedy of Madame Bovary* (Jermyn Street Theatre); *The Unlocked Door* (Seaton Delaval Hall with November Club); *The Wasp* (Customs House); *A Midsummer Night's Dream* (Reading Rep); *Hound of the Baskervilles* (East Riding Theatre); *The Remarkable Robin Armstrong's Extraordinary Christmas Adventure* (Hexham Theatre); *Legend of Sleepy Hollow* (UK Tour); *Hound of the Baskervilles* (Northern Stage); *Good Timin, West End Girls* (Live Theatre); *Story Project Rage, Romance and Resolution, Miss Havisham's Wedding Night* and *12 Poems of Emily Dickinson* (Arcola Theatre); *Grand Hotel, Lend Me a Tenor, 9 to 5, King of Hearts* (London School of Musical Theatre), *Spaced 2014* (Touchpaper Theatre).

Me Lost Me aka Jayne Dent

Composer/musician

Jayne Dent is an interdisciplinary artist, musician, composer and facilitator based in Newcastle upon Tyne, predominantly working with sound; recording, improvising and performing with electronics and voice, while additionally incorporating elements of textiles, writing, digital art, interactive installation, moving image and print. History, mythology and landscape are common themes throughout her work, with a particular focus on exploring the intersection between folk art and developing technology: what stories will be told and how will we tell them in the future? Her work often highlights and connects through-lines from ancient cultures to the present day, and uses this as a basis to dream and speculate on what is to come, with a keen interest in experimenting with modes of storytelling, from the literal to the surreal and the abstract. Her experimental songwriting project under moniker 'Me Lost Me' has been described in The Guardian as 'stripping folk back to its bones while letting its future echoes bleed out', a beguiling mix of soaring vocals and atmospheric electronics that playfully push the boundaries of genre. With her prolific writing and extensive touring schedule, her unique sound has won much support across the musical spectrum. Dent has notably performed live for BBC Radio 3's After Dark Festival and as part of the 2022 BBC Proms alongside Spell Songs, Royal Northern Sinfonia and the Voices of the Rivers Edge Choir. She received the prestigious Paul Hamlyn Foundation Award for Composers and was 2020–21 Artist in Residence at Sage Gateshead. Her third album 'RPG', released in July 2023 on Upset the Rhythm, was MOJO Magazine's 4* Folk Album of the Month, who described the release as 'Incomprehensible/ Irresistible', while The Quietus dubbed it 'A celebration of the essentially human playfulness of gaming, storytelling and songs'.

David Flynn

Associate Sound Designer

David trained in media production before working in theatre, events and live music as a sound engineer and AV technician. He is currently Technical Manager for Live Theatre, one of the UK's leading new writing theatres renowned for producing and presenting new plays. David is also a freelance sound designer. Sound design credits include: *Educating Rita* (national tour/Theatre by the Lake/David Pugh); *One Off* (Live Theatre); *Clear White Light, My Romantic History* (Olivier nominated), *The Red Lion* (Live Theatre/Trafalgar Studio's London); *The Savage, Harriet Martineau Dreams of Dancing, Flying into Daylight, Wet House* (Live Theatre/Hull Truck/Soho Theatre); *Cooking with Elvis, Faith and Cold Reading, A Walk on Part* (Live Theatre/Soho Theatre/Arts Theatre London); *A Northern Odyssey*.

Drummond Orr

Lighting Designer/Production Manager

Drummond has over forty years' experience as a theatre electrician, technical manager, lighting designer and production manager. In that time, he has toured nationally and internationally, and has worked in both touring and production theatre.

Lighting design credits include: *The Cold Buffet* (Live Theatre)*; Love It If We Beat Them* (Live Theatre); *One Off* (Live Theatre); *The Red Lion* (Live Theatre/Trafalgar Studios); *My Romantic History, The Savage, Cooking With Elvis* and *Wet House* (Live Theatre/Hull Truck/Soho Theatre); *Tyne, The Prize, Nativities, Two Pints* and *A Walk On Part*

(LiveTheatre/Soho Theatre/Arts Theatre); *Blackbird* (Market Theatre, Johannesburg); *The Girl in the Yellow Dress* (Market Theatre, Johannesburg/Grahamstown Festival/Baxter Theatre, Cape Town/ Citizens, Glasgow); *Educating Rita* (Theatre by the Lake/David Pugh and UK tour).

About Live Theatre

'*One of the most fertile crucibles of new writing*' **The Guardian**

Our vision is for a North East that writes its own story and fights for a more creative future.

Live Theatre occupies a unique place as one of the country's only dedicated new writing buildings outside of London. Across its fifty-year history it has launched the careers of many of today's leading theatre figures and continues to develop and platform the artists of tomorrow, from playwrights to local school children. Deeply connected to its region and unafraid to confront the most pressing issues of our time, Live Theatre brings ambitious regional artists and adventurous local audiences into vivid contact.

Our mission is to unearth the rich and unexpected narratives of our region, to nurture creativity and bring passionate ideas to life and to be a space that unites people and ignites imaginations.

'*Live Theatre has supported generation after generation of new writers, actors and theatre artists.*' **Lee Hall, Playwright**

To learn more about Live Theatre and get involved see www.live.org.uk

Live Theatre in partnership with Smart Works.

#ActsofLove

As part of *Three Acts of Love*, Live Theatre is proud to be collaborating with **Smart Works** and are holding a Clothing Drive for the entirety of the shows run. **Smart Works Newcastle** is a UK charity that dresses and coaches unemployed women in preparation for a job interview. Bring along your high-quality clothing donations during Box Office hours and you will be helping Smart Works to change the trajectory of another woman's life. For more information on the clothing drive and how you can help visit smartworks.org.uk.

Best Friends

Noreen Bates
Jim Beirne
Michael and Pat Brown
George Caulkin
Helen Coyne
Christine Elton
Chris Foy
Robson Green
Brenna Hobson
John Jordan
Graham Maddick

Elaine Orrick
Paul Shevlin
Margaret and John Shipley
Shelagh Stephenson
Sting
Alan Tailford
Edward Walker-Fraser
David Walton
Sue Wilson
Lucy Winskell

Good Friends

Vincent Allen
John Appleton
Jeff and Susan Brown
Alec Collerton
Ron Cook
Joe Douglas
Ross Freeman
Ann Gittins
Eileen Jones
John Mason
Rhys McKinnell
David Nellist

Chris Connell and Lucy Nichol
Linda Norris
Michelle Percy
Pat Ritchie
Martin Saunders
Phil Skingley
Susan and Mike Stewart
John Stokel-Walker
John Tomaney
Angela Walton
K F Walton
Mary and Steve Wootten

Friends

Pat Allcorn
Sharon Austin
Norma Banfi
Bex Bowsher
Lynn Boyes
Lawrence Bryson
Rob Chapman
Sally-Anne Cooper
Angela Cooper
Judy Cowgill
Glynis Downie
Suky Drummond
Keith Elliott
Sue Emmas
Robert Fairfax

David Fenwick
Carolyn Ford
Joanna Foster
John Graham
Julie Grant
Moira Gray
Dorothy Hair
Gael Henry
Ruth and Robert Heyman
Gillian Hitchenes
Wendy Holland
Irene Hudson
Beverley Jewitt
Richard Kain
Nicole Kavanagh-Stubbs

John Loughlin
Gen Lowes
Stephanie Malyon
Sarah Marshall
Michael McBride
Ian Mowbray
Linda Moss
Stepanie O'Connor
Jean Ollerton
Clare Overton
Jonathan Pye
David Robertson
Jo Robinson
Julian Rogan

Jean Scott
Jill Scrimshaw
Alan and Rosalind Share
Monica Shaw
Jo Shepherd
Ian and Christine Shepherdson
Tracey Sinclair
Brent Taylorson
Don Tennet
Robert Vardill
Sandra Wake
Sue Ward
Keith Williamson

Plus those who choose to remain anonymous.

Live Theatre Staff

Executive Director/Joint Chief Executive	**Jacqui Kell**
Artistic Director/Joint Chief Executive	**Jack McNamara**
PA to Joint Chief Executives	**Alex Readman**

Creative Programme

New Work Producer	**JD Stewart**
Projects Producer	**John Dawson**
Associate Artists	**gobscure**
	Kemi-Bo Jacobs

Children and Young People

CYPP Leader	**Helen Green**
Senior Creative Associate CYPP	**Paul James**
CYPP Administrator	**Amy Foley**
Creative Lead Live Tales	**Becky Morris**

Technical Production

Production Manager	**Drummond Orr**
Technical and Digital Manager	**David Flynn**
Technician	**Taylor Howie**
Estates and Maintenance Assistant	**Ken Evans**

Operations and Finance

Finance Manager	**Antony Robertson**
Finance and Payroll Officer	**Catherine Moody**
Fundraising and Development Manager	**Alison Nicholson**

Marketing and Communications

Marketing and Communications Manager	**Lisa Campbell**
Marketing and Communications Manager	**Michele McCallion**
Marketing and Communications Officer	**Arthur Roberts**

Customer Services and Box Office

Customer Services and Estate Manager	**Ben Young**
Duty Manager	**Michael Davies**
Duty Manager and Bar Supervisor	**Alicia Meehan**
Duty Manager and Bar Supervisor	**Sarah Matthews**
Duty Manager and Bar Supervisor	**Patrycja Nowacka**
Duty Manager and Bar Supervisor	**Jake Wilson Craw**
Bar Supervisor	**Fay Carrington**
Customer Services Assistant	**Elisha Ewing**
Customer Services Assistant	**Caitlin Fairlamb**
Customer Services Assistant	**Brennan Flanders**
Customer Services Assistant	**Elspeth Frith**
Customer Services Assistant	**Joel Houghton**
Customer Services Assistant	**Lukas Gabrysch**
Customer Services Assistant	**Alicja Gadomski**
Customer Services Assistant	**Joe Kell**
Customer Services Assistant	**Bridget Marumo**
Customer Services Assistant	**Kathryn Watt**
Box Office Assistant	**Daniel Ball**
Box Office Assistant	**Asa Beckett**
Box Office Assistant	**Steven Blackshaw**
Box Office Assistant	**Joseph Duffy**
Box Office Assistant	**Ruby Taylor**
Box Office Assistant	**Hannah Sparkes**
Box Office Assistant	**Jasper Wilding**
Box Office Assistant	**Joseph Duffy**

Housekeeping

Housekeeping	**Lydia Igbinosa**
Housekeeping	**Jean Kent**
Housekeeping	**Angela Salem**
Housekeeping	**Camille Vitorino-Itoua**

The Start of Space

Laura Lindow

It is compassion – that moves us beyond numbness toward healing.

Chekhov

Writer's Note

The world of this play and all characters and events are fictional. Whilst inspired by observations of the medical world and all its beautiful, complicated realities, the characters' experiences, voices and journeys are imagined. Any similarities to any actual persons or real events are accidental.

The World of the Play

*Throughout the piece power-point slides could be presented to title or illustrate the sections. When formal lecture gives way the slides seem to have a life of their own and transform to become **Ellie**'s drawings.*

*The character of the **Child** should be played in earnest, without condescension. **Rory** can be played either by a live actor or using recorded voice. He is a beloved haunting.*

***Sophie** should be voiced by **McGill**.*

Finally, this is written as a love story and celebration of life. Staging should be minimal and the emotional journey played for honesty. Without overt sentimentality, but with heart.

***Finally:** Dedicated to all heart heroes on both sides of the deal, and to those who support. And to Sarah Napuk. I hope she flew.*

A woman walks onto the stage. She is wet from snow outside.

She is **Dr Fiona McGill**. *Aged late 40s she is here to give a presentation. A lecture.*

Impressive at first glance. Smartly dressed at first glance. A successful woman. At first glance.

We are in the large lecture theatre at the Royal Victoria Infirmary, Newcastle.

McGill (*audience*) Come in, come in.

Can you hear me at the back? Phones off please if you wouldn't mind.

And thank you for your patience, while we set up. And I locate my notes. I'm glad you found your way here. The RVI can be a maze if you're not familiar.

I apologise for my appearance. (*Wet through.*)

The snow. As you will have gathered those of you from farther afield, the Newcastle weather is predictably unpredictable. Right. Notes.

McGill *checks pockets. Finds cards.*

Bit soggy, but . . .
(*Reading.*) Hello. My name is Dr McGill, as you know from your course information, and I have been a cardiothoracic surgeon for the last . . . well . . . for a lifetime it seems. Meaning . . . Hearts mainly. It's my job to know hearts.

I'm here with you to present a lecture on . . . share my own findings around . . . well on this cold winter's evening, together hopefully we will come out of this event with a little more insight on that which makes us tick. If we can achieve that then . . . I think we can agree we are . . . we are winning. I'll do my best.

So. Cardiology. 'A branch of medicine that deals with diseases and abnormalities of the heart.' The Heart Department my son used to call it.

Over the last century, there has been unimaginable progress in what is still a relatively young field. Matters of the heart have never been faster paced so to speak.

We know more and can *do* more. Things that we would have believed impossible. We can predict. We can prevent. We can mend. We can exchange one for the other. A poor for a healthy. Even in the smallest of babies, which is my speciality. Paediatrics. Children.

Beat.

We can save and extend life. And we do. We try to offer quality of days *and* quantity of days. And we're getting better at it. At helping people to . . . live. Or should be. Slide please?

Slide: Diagram of heart (the last slide that will look scientific)

There it is. Our mothership. Most vital organ in the centre of the body pumping litres of blood through a network of arteries and veins. It is placed . . . (*Gestures.*) here. As adults it weighs around eight to twelve ounces dependent on the size of the human and is (I'd encourage you to make notes) and is at birth the size of a walnut, when grown the size of a fist. (*Shows us.*) A clenched fist. Try it.

We cannot live without its function. We cannot function.

Beat.

Aristotle called it the centre of nerves. Galen's 'source of heat'. The organ 'closest to the soul'. 'A good heart is the sun and moon. Or rather the sun not the moon for it shines bright and never changes' – Shakespeare. **Never changes!**

As you'll know, made up of four chambers, the left and the right ventricle, left and right atriums and four valves, and believe it or not, whether you are a saint or a sinner, our hearts, when healthy, look pretty much the same as one another. No pearls of wisdom buried inside. No golden glow of goodness, no rotten core nor dark secrets lurking. No shadows of intent. No treasure.

Just flesh and fibre. It's as simple and as furious as that.
Sorry to disappoint.

I'm not religious, but the genius and the jeopardy, the
terrible beauty . . . astounds me. Confounds me. As it does
us all, and will no doubt continue to ad infinitum. However
clever you or I think we get.

Beat.

What does it take to be a heart surgeon? Anyone? (*Wryly.*)
Steady hands?

Plus of course communication, spatial awareness, good
problem solving . . . A children's heart surgeon? All of the
above, and more.

Find the problem. Fix the problem. With whatever resources
are available to you. That is what drives us, yes?
But what if . . . what if the problem is you? How do you fix
that?

The **Child** *enters. Dressed in pyjamas.* **McGill** *doesn't look.*

What about when you've hardly slept for nights on end and
you are numb and weary as the world is old?

When helping others is the last thing on your mind?! When
all you can think of is /

Child   Spaghetti hoops?

McGill   / all you can think is when you might stop. There is
such expectation for research and lectures . . . To give back.
To continually move us forward. At pace.
Like tonight giving talks to future doctors. (*Gestures to
audience.*)

We are a small number.
And I am an even rarer specimen. One of seven female heart
surgeons. In the country. (*quickly*) Don't google that.

What is the difference between a heart surgeon and God?
Anyone?
God doesn't think he is a heart surgeon.

It's true. Cardio surgeons are the only practitioners who have the legal power to stop and to start a heartbeat at will. If anyone must be more certain, more *sure* of themselves . . . it is we. You have to believe *you can do this*.

Every decision a crucial junction. And of course none you make alone. You have a trusted team around you. But that first cut into a human chest. The knife in *your* hand. You're on your own.
It takes faith. One wrong move can mean /

Child   / Baked beans?

McGill   And if that goes . . . (*Looks at* **Child**.) Every failure is an injury. (*Looks at hands.*)

Child   What about Marmite? I'm asking. Marmite?

McGill (*ignoring her*)   There will of course be a chance for you to ask anything at the end.

The secret is to breathe.
And remember, the job is about *life*. Death is an essential companion. The other side of the deal. But it *is life* that is our interest.

It started to snow when I was on my way here. I walked through the park. I love this city in the snow. This building. Look, I had prepared . . . but my notes. Wet through and useless . . . maybe I could talk to you. Just talk.

(*Not reading.*)

How does it feel? I've had the privilege to hold over a hundred hearts here in my hands. I've helped and I've hindered.

Beat.

(*To self.*) How *does* it feel?

Child   Are you going to talk about me now?

McGill (*to* **Child**)   Yes. Yes I am. Why don't you get back
into your bed.
I'm going to tell it.
(*To us.*) This time last year. I am late. I am never late. Slide
please.

Slide – a child's drawing of a spaceship appears.

McGill *stares at it.*

Child *gets into bed as the atmosphere changes. We are in hospital.*
McGill *holds arms out as though being scrubbed, putting on apron,
removing gloves, the ballet that she does.*

2022

*Hospital sounds: Have you got / are we in time for the / the team is
ready for / if you could prepare the patient then we can get them up
as soon as we /*

McGill (*to us*)   I have no surgery today but I still have the
HDU round to do, Clinic to visit and a lecture to give . . . I'm
against the clock. I'm always against the clock. I remember
the day because /

'Good morning everyone.' We're a fair crowd. The whole
multi-disciplinary team, with a cluster of students following
on like a shoal of fish. I'm keen to get finished as soon as I
can. I have a letter in my pocket. I remember this day
because this is the day . . . I am going to resign.

We move from space to space, talking quietly. Visitors.
Reassuring. Updating. Pausing to corroborate and
recommend.

Each bed is a snapshot. Bubbles of home. Fragments of
whole lives, kidnapped from their day to days and
transported into this scrubbed universe. Sometimes with no
warning.

In this ward, patients waiting for transplant can be there, in one room, in one bed for hours, days, mostly months . . . Sometimes years.

We are almost finished the round. Just one cubicle to go.

(*Reads.*) Complex history with recent deterioration. Extra support required.

Ah yes. I remember this. Has anyone met patient and family yet? No?

'Transferred from Glasgow this morning' says the Cardiologist. (**McGill** *checks notes.*) Right.

McGill (*entering space; to* **Child**)   'Hello. I'm Dr McGill. This is the team. In you come everyone. Patient won't bite. This must be . . .' (*A long expectant pause.*) 'Must be . . .'

Child *is lying in the bed with a cardboard box balanced over her head.*

Child (*from under the box*)   An astronaut.

McGill (*to* **Child** *in a tone supposedly suited to speaking to a child*) 'An astronaut, hey?'

Child   S'right.

McGill (*to* **Child**)   Well, welcome back to Earth. To Newcastle.
Is this a picture of your spaceship? I hope you've paid for parking. (*To us.*) Hahahaha. The students laugh politely.

Child   I don't have a spaceship. I'm seven. I came in an ambulance.

McGill (*to* **Child**)   'So you did. (*Tries again.*) I like your pyjamas. Or is it a space suit? A space suit with pom poms?'

Child   Pyjamas.

McGill (*to* **Child**)   I see.

(*To us.*) She is smaller than her age suggests, her toes only reach halfway down the bed. The juniors are staring.

(*To* **Child**.) What does your box say? (*Reads upside down writing.*) This Way Up. (*To us.*) More laughs from the students.

Child (*stung*)   It's a helmet. I need it to breathe. The atmosphere is poison.

McGill *rubs eyes. She reaches forward and opens the flap at the front of the helmet*

McGill (*to* **Child**)   Hello in there. Anyone home?

Child   Fuck. Off.

McGill   What the . . .?! Did she just say . . .?! (*Closes flap sharply. To us.*) I've had enough. Last night's wine is bearing down on my forehead along with the hours of sleep I didn't get.

(*Calls to the air.*) Claire . . .?

(*To us.*) You'll find that there are staff members you rely on more than others. Play Specialists. Worth their weight.

(*To an imagined colleague.*) Off sick? Is Mum around? Or Dad? No? For God's . . . It's SO frustrating when the parents jump ship on arrival. She's clearly struggling. And the last thing that we need is /

Child   / I hate Newcastle. Don't talk about me when I'm right here.

Beat.

McGill (*to* **Child**)   I thought you were inside your helmet.

Child   I can still hear you.

McGill   'It . . . it is made of cardboard' points out one of the students. Reasonably.

Yes. (*Stops for a beat. Then to the* **Child**.) I'll come back.

Child Don't bother! I don't want you.

McGill (*to us*) I leave the student fish who are either about to blow actual bubbles or who are trying not to laugh. For real.

I'm too tired today. In fact I can't think when I wasn't too tired. On call over three nights and every other weekend.

When I'm at home, I sleep in a chair. My wife upstairs. It's been that way for years.
Our living room is dusty. Large windows look out onto a shared green.
Our roses grow wild.
They look after themselves do roses. I always had them down as sensitive but . . . Tenacious.
The nights are noisy. Traffic in the distance. My mother's kitchen clock. The dripping tap in the downstairs toilet. My breathing. And the missing footsteps that whisper on the floorboards above my head. Since our boy flew our nest.

Slide – a child's drawing of a whirlwind

Memory 2017

Rory *enters in a whirlwind.*

McGill Rory! Stop thundering! I'm busy, the door was closed. Where's the fire? What do you want?

Rory I'm in a hurry. I'm going. Now. Had you forgotten?

McGill (*lying*) Course not. (*Then.*) What time's your train?

Rory I'm not getting the train.

McGill Oh I can't take you. I'm sorry, love. I've got /

Rory / Mam's giving me a lift. You've got the car key?

McGill Right. (*Stands up on awkward ceremony.*) So what's first on the agenda?

Rory   I've got the itinerary printed on the fridge. Have you had a look.

McGill   Not yet, but I will.
(*Rallying*.) How do you feel? Are you nervous? Excited?

Rory   I'm late. You're busy. And I'm back at the weekend. Key? Thanks, Mam.

McGill   Don't I get a . . . (**Rory** *comes back, pecks* **McGill,** *and goes. She is left to call after him.*) Have a wonderful . . . I know you'll have a . . . Go get 'em.

Silence. He's gone. She shuts the door.

Present

Remembering

McGill   I know what you see.
I am fifty years old.
But I have a long memory.
At twenty-one I was a student. I met my wife, Sophie.
On placement, both of us. She in the year above so different circles, but when we passed each other, I . . . noticed.

I've always been myself. Never in doubt about who I am.
Who I will love. I could tell you about the hard times. The fear. The fight. But I'd rather tell you about the part kept hidden from most of the heterosexual world. The joy.

I am out and proud by default. Easy to read. Or was.
From adolescence bumping from love to love. An ungainly and irresponsible pilot.

The placements terrify me at first. But you soon find it's invigorating to be in the thick of it. *Real* patients. *Real* cases.
Specialists you can worship and scrutinise in the flesh.
My opinion . . . my *knowledge* starts to mean something.
From 'Don't ask me anything' to 'Ask me, I know'.

I don't think I pay attention to anything or anyone around
me. Until . . .

She has a laugh you can't mistake. And talks to everyone.
Impressive, that's the word.
Whizzing down the corridors. Loud. Upright. Me, earnest,
invisible. She, a force.
And her ears . . . Odd commas either side. Like she's living
inside ironic quotation marks.
I don't think ears alone should be a recommendation on
someone's character, but this particular set imply . . . I don't
know . . . fun.

'Sexy geek', she says of me when we compare notes after the
fact. And then something about my decisive forearms. (!!)

Slide – child's drawing of comets colliding

Our eventual collision is down a stairway, dark and sweaty.
Smelling of piss and poppers. Loud music and a heavy beat.
End of year night out. It's late. It's messy.
Lights strobe. The crowd heave in jerks.

Not my natural habitat. But after eight whiskies, I know I'm
alive. Balanced on a skinny stool by the bar.
Inwardly channelling Humphrey Bogart.
Looking like a pissed Terry Nutkins.
I'm on the water. By necessity.

She's been dancing. Flops down on the seat next to mine.

'Hello,' she says.

McGill   She's looking at me like I'm a puzzle.
Fresh skin and wide mouth.
She smells like salt sea breeze and late nights . . . Or the
other way round.

Sophie   I know you.

McGill   She is speaking into my ear for the music. I breathe
in her warmth.

I'm heating up under her green gaze. Hands sweating.
'From the hospital? Pleased to /'

Sophie   You've been looking at me.

McGill   Was I? Have I? Told you. Easy to read. 'I'm sorry. I
didn't think . . . Can I get you . . . Would you like a / drink'

Sophie   / Do you know what I've been wondering?

McGill   Oh god.

She's leathered. Takes my beaker of tap water and downs it
like . . . sexy tequila.

Sophie   I'm wondering, what would happen if I kiss you?

McGill   I have no idea. 'I have no idea,' I say. She pulls her
seat close. A pulse starts in my cheek. Wondering if I look as
though I'm panicking. I can't feel my feet.
She is so close. Touches my arm.

Sophie   Shall we find out?

McGill   Maybe we should / not? Too late.

She closes her eyes. I brace for impact. Her wide mouth
meets mine, my world bursts into life, the floor goes from
underneath, and we tip from those bar stools into the rest of
our lives.

**Slide – child's colourful diagram: pie chart of 'hospital
athmosfere'.**

**Broken down as: 'big chunk – fish fingers. Little chunk –
cleaning stuff. Another little chunk – sweaty feet. The rest
– worry'.**

McGill   Notorious, isn't it?
But to me hospital air is thick with treatment and recovery.

Back in my student days if you'd told me I would be looking
to give it all up . . . I'd call you a liar.

2022

McGill   'We've made a plan'. This is the transplant coordinator.

'A behaviour plan. Claire's still off and Mam keeps going AWOL, hardly around to support. We are talking about the box. The psychologist has been in, but we're all concerned. She's still refusing any engagement. The team say treating her is nigh on impossible'.
It's a dangerous game.
'So the approach is go gently. Don't show that you're fazed. Whatever she says. Gently'. To me, 'You're up McGill. See what you can do.
And don't try to force it.
I mean it. She bit the teacher. Hard.'

McGill (*wary*)   They said you'd been asking for me? (*Helpfully.*) The one with a face like a horse?

Child (*No reply.*)

McGill (*to* **Child**)   I'm pleased to see you. The one with a face like a . . . box (*Trails off. Silence.*) We need to talk.

Child *turns their back.*

Well, while we're getting to know each other . . .

(*To us.*) I try making my pencil wiggle.

Child   Rubbish.

McGill (*to* **Child**)   Woops. Have you seen my glasses?

Child   On your head.

McGill (*to* **Child**)   Hey look at that! One arm is longer than the /

(*To us.*) Have you ever seen cardboard show disdain? Powerful. Lastly . . .

(*To* **Child**.) Is there a patient under that box? Can I lift it up and say Hell / o

Child   / No! It's mine. I need it. So you just *get fucked.*

McGill (*to* **Child**)   Wow. Where did you . . . That is not the kind of . . . I just wanted to talk to you about /

Child   I know what you're going to say.

McGill (*to* **Child**)   Just to explain a few things . . . (*Aside.*) Where the hell is Mum?! (*To us.*) My patience was wearing /

(*To* **Child**.) You know you have a very poorly /

Child   No.

McGill (*to* **Child**)   And when we can we're going to give you an operation that will /

Child   No

McGill (*to* **Child**)   But it is crucial that you take your medic /

Child   *You* take your medication.

McGill (*to* **Child**, *rising*)   I don't have any . . . It is for your own . . . we are trying to make sure your body has all of the /

Child   / Whoosh.

McGill (*confused beat; to* **Child**)   'What was that'?

Child   Hatch closed. I can't hear you. So you might as well fuck off.

McGill (*to* **Child**)   There is a hospital policy that we don't have to put up with verbal abuse even if it is from a seven-year-old. You can mind your manners, and listen to what I have to say, or . . . (*Trying to think of suitable threat.*)

Child   Or what?

McGill (*to us*)   Suddenly I'm angry. Furious. (*To* **Child**.) Or you can just *fuck right off* yourself.

A pause.

(*To us.*) The word 'gently' floats past my eyes.

Another pause.

Child   Over.

McGill   ???

Child   Say 'over'. Then I can hear you. 'Fuck off over.'

McGill   Fuck o . . . No, listen. I'm not going to say it again. I'm sorry. I've had a bad day. A bad week.

Child   You shouldn't swear at children.

McGill   You're right. Although you did say it first.

Pause.

Child   I don't think your arm is longer than that one. I think that was a trick

McGill   Clever.

Child   I am clever. I need to tell you some things. They said you'd be the one to talk to. That you're the one that does all the . . . (*hand to chest, earnestly*) you know what's.

McGill   I'm listening.

Child   BUT you'll need to pass my test.
Then the hatch'll open.

McGill   OK. (*Surreptitiously looks at watch.*) Try me.

Child   What's your actual name?

McGill   Fiona.

Child   Have you got a family? Are you married?

McGill   Yes. And yes.

Child   Children?

McGill   Yes. One.

Child   What does your husband do?

McGill   She's a doctor too.

Child   She?

McGill   Yes.

Pause.

Child   Is that possible?! To marry a girl?

McGill   Lots of things are possible. Any astronaut worth their salt knows that.

Pause.

Child   Yes.

McGill   Will you take off your helmet?

Child   Is it safe?

McGill   Yes. I'm the expert remember?

Child *doesn't.*

Child   Three things I need to tell you. I don't want an operation. Thank you. I don't want a new heart. I like my one. Second, my mam's not missing. She's worried is all. She gets stressed. Doesn't like hospitals.

McGill   OK. Right. And third?

Child   Will you give me your wiggly pen?! Over.

McGill   Three years after we meet, Sophie and I, we have a baby.
Our new baby is awake for four of the six hours available to us. I'm able to tune the sound out. Sophie is not. She's knackered.
And apparently I am not helping.

The timetable of a GP and an ambitious consultant back then are not sympathetic to parenting a child. Overwork. Stress. Lack of sleep.

At the time I'm young. I can take it. I am good at it even. Compartmentalising. And I am working my way through the ranks. Huge amounts of travel, work and study. Learning my craft.

'I'm a knot', he'll say to me further down the line, crossing his legs and wrapping his arms tight around. 'I'm a human knot. Try and undo me, Mam.' I can't.

Sophie says our son adores me – copies me, taking on my mannerisms.

Granted you can see a bit of me in his frown. And sometimes when he's filling his nappy. I try not to take it personally. When he smiles of course he is all her. He has her ears.

Memory

2018

We hear a distant phone ring.

Rory   Hi. Mam?

McGill   Rory? Hi. How's it going?

Rory   It's OK.

McGill   What's happening? Working hard?

Rory   Yup.

McGill   How's the course?

Rory   Yeh. Interesting. Hard.

McGill   So? You called. I'm just phoning back.

Rory   I didn't.

McGill   You did. I have a missed call.

Rory   No. Check the date.

She does.

McGill   Ah. Sorry. Was it important?

Rory   No. I got sorted.

McGill   Your Mam mentioned you'd been a bit stressed out. Is it the exams? Sophie said I should check in with you?

Was that why you called? Because you know I'm always here.
We both are.

Rory   I'm OK.

McGill   You sure?

You know you can always call if you need anything. I mean I
know you did. But you know you can again. And I'll get
straight back. When I see it. Rory, I'm sorry.

Rory   No. You're OK.

McGill   Sure? OK. Hang on in there. You can do it. Eye on
the prize. I love you.

Present

Remembering

McGill   When the hospital doors pull shut the world out
there need not exist. I am different when I'm inside these
walls. I can be useful.
When Rory is younger he believes I live in the railway
station because they drop me there so often, bags in hand.
Off to look after other people's children.
And he grows.
Running and running. Even when he's walking he looks like
he's running, like a comedy character, knees bent, elbows
out, chin forward. Following his busy little back I'm wracked
with all the horrible things that could happen to him. Every
pavement is too narrow. Every staircase too high. That
terrible love. That fear and worry that is stitched all the way
through.

'Let him find his way. He's an adventurer,' Sophie says. I
can't stand it.

Sophie says I use work to hide from responsibility. I say that
she is jealous of my growing career. She says I'm an arsehole.

She's right of course.

But we hang on together in our spinning universe,

Crumbs and bickering spilling out as we go,
as we career from day to day and month to month.
We manage. Together for all those years we manage. Until
we don't.
Until the twentieth of November 2018.

2022

McGill *is making notes having just completed the ward round.*

Child   It was my birthday last week.

McGill   That's a coincidence – mine is next week.

Child   I was eight.

McGill   I'll be forty-nine.

Child (*appalled*)   Woah. I'm sorry. I'll make you a present?

McGill   I should make you one. Did you get anything nice?

Child   Got this.

Child *reaches for a shiny new book from the bedside.*

McGill (*looks at the book and reads title*)   'The Start of Space
and other Fascinating Facts.' (*Sounding impressed.*) Well!

Child   From Claire.

McGill   Right.

Child   Yes. My class phoned on Facetime. But I was busy.

Do you like it?

McGill   I do. I like facts.

Child   Say stop. (*Flicks through the book.*)

McGill   Stop.

Child (*reads*) 'History and The World.
Did cavemen hunt dinosaurs? (*Without stopping.*) No. They
existed at different times.'
Say stop. (*Flicks again.*)

McGill Stop.

Child (*reads*) 'What would you do in the Dead Sea?'

McGill Fl /

Child 'Float'. You're not doing very well. Tell me
something you know but I don't.

McGill I could tell you a lot about your heart.

Child (*quickly*) Too easy.

McGill (*to us*) Makes you wonder why I trained . . .

(*To* **Child**.) It's amazing you know it beats about one
hundred thousand times a day! There are three thousand
five hundred individual anomalies / and

Child No, not hearts. That's boring. (*Wide eyed.*) What
about space.

McGill Alright. How about . . . (*Thinks.*) The first people
on the moon. Their footprints will be there for years to
come. Millions of years. Because?

Child I don't know.

McGill No gravity. An adventurer taught me that.

Beat.

Child How does gravity mean footprints stay?

McGill I don't know. Dust I suppose. Nothing to move it
around.

Child (*starts to laugh*) Just thinking . . . next time someone's
there they'll go . . . Is someone following me? Bigfoot? A
space ghost? Then people in NASA will go 'eh?' There'll be
things on the news about the moon space ghost. (*Laughs.*)

Then they'll turn round and go 'who's there' and it's their own footprints . . . and (*Laughs and laughs.*)

Slide – a child's drawing of a NASA specialist with a telescope saying 'amayzing!'

McGill   Babies' veins are as thin and fragile as hairs. Can you imagine? Every chest cavity a complex network of crucial connections and pulsing intricacies. They look so delicate. But small people, they are tough. They look to live.

And me? My demeanour might be clumsy, my thumbs might not be agile enough to send a text message at any respectable speed . . . or chop an onion in a minute. But when I'm in amongst it, my hands belong to a precision artist. A musician. An engineer. It all makes sense. My fingers, mind and body, work.

Some surgeons picture the patient when they are operating. Some say that the relationship, the care they feel is a crucial part of what helps them to do their job. Me? I have always thought of it as a technical exercise. Against the clock. I could do it so well precisely because . . . I know how this sounds . . . but I could do it for all of those years *because* I left my emotions at the door. Tell me what sort of quality is that?!

Capable yet cack-handed in equal measure, these hands. They have stitched in a thousand chests. And yet when it matters most these hands are incompetent to the last.

Past

A phone rings in the distance.

McGill   November 2018.

Sophie   He didn't come home.

McGill   Sophie's worried.
I'm furious.

'*Idiot,*' I say. 'What an irresponsible idiot.'
'It isn't like him', Sophie says, quietly.

Rory makes me rage harder than I thought anyone could.
People don't warn you about that.

Sophie says I have unrealistic expectations.
He always says I don't understand him.
That no one understands him.
I say he's being dramatic.

His absence says otherwise.

I see it on the ward like I've got x-ray vision. Naked wires of
parental worry that criss-cross around the hospital beds
netted like woven cloud. Useless but live. Charged with
panic and fret. The tiny shoulders in the centre of it trying
not to set anything off. Trying to take care of the adults
around.
I see it. I know it. I look the other way in case I feel it.

Rory gives me his all and I have no idea what to do with it.
No idea how to look after it. In life and in death.

2022

Slide – child's drawing. A crocodile holding a clock.

Child   Is it really going to happen?

McGill   It has to.

Child   When?

McGill   As soon as we can. Days, or weeks, or months.
Could be tonight.

Child   You definitely can't put it in through my nose?

McGill   Through your chest.

Child   Ouch.

McGill   You'll be asleep.

Child   Promise?

McGill   Yep. You'll wake up with it all done. And you'll feel better.

Child   Can I keep my old heart?

McGill   No.

Child   What will you do with it?

McGill   We have a look at it to see if there's anything we can learn. And then we'll have to throw it away.
But you are helping. Just like someone is really helping you by giving you theirs.

Child   They won't know. They'll be dead.

McGill   Their family will know.
They will be pleased to know that someone like you is looking after it.

Child (*whispers*)   Will I die? Over?

McGill (*falsely indignant*)   I do hope not. I'll do my best. (*then softer*) The numbers say definitely probably no way. Fact.

Child   Right.

McGill   You have an even better chance if you work with us. And when it's time, we'll be able to join forces. You know, the medicine you'll be on is like a superpower. Means when it happens your body won't think it has to fight the new heart, like it's . . . an alien.

Child   Trick it?

McGill   Yes. Honestly. (*Beat.*) You know you could die if we don't do everything we can. Over.

Child   Did you know that a bumble bee can't actually fly? It's against physics? (*Pause.*) Can I choose the colour thread you use?

McGill   It's a special see-through thread.

Child   Will you warm up your hands before you do it?

McGill (*to us*)   .. says Ellie. (*To* **Child**.) You'll be asleep. You won't feel a thing. Fact.

(*To us*.) She doesn't answer. Just ties the tie of her dressing gown tight, like it's made of stern stuff and nods.

(*To* **Child**.) I know it's scary, (*To us*.) I say. I do know.

Child   I'm going to think of it like an adventure.

The **Child** *takes off her cardboard box helmet.*

OK.

McGill   OK. Tell me something else I don't know.

Child   I don't know anything.

McGill   Yes you do. Have a think.

Child   OK. (*Looks at book.*) My favourite. What is sixty-two miles away?

McGill   I don't know.

Child   The start of space.

McGill   The start of space.

McGill (*to herself*)   Sixty-two miles. Yes. Of course it is. (*Repeats.*) The start of space.

Child   You know they probably might learn something new. From my heart. Bet you've never seen an astronaut's heart before. You might find treasure. Or a new kind of bone. Over and out.

Present

Remembering

2018. Sixty-two miles away from here. His fuzzy image caught on the CCTV. Taken from a camera angle I'd never seen, from above his head looking down. Unmistakable ears. His orange cagoule. Elbows out. Knees bent. Chin up. Anyone else might have thought he was running. Sixty-two miles away. Berwick station. The last time he was seen. Posted all over social media. Aged Nineteen. Vulnerable. Have you seen him. Rory McGill.

I'd had no idea he was lost.

I want to reach into each screen to take back hold of the fuzzy figure. Pull him close. To safety.

McGill   Sophie and I turn into an imprint of something once living. Now coiled, carved and fossilised.

The air between us unmoved.
Our boy's footprints safe from gravity.

As the numbness sets in.

My body knows to keep moving.
Minute to minute. Day to day
but that day, in November 2018, my heart . . . stopped.
I go and stand under that camera, amongst those leaves.
Trying to catch his shadow. But my hands . . . the air is empty. And he is still gone. And all I can see when I look back is the distance.
How can I have missed him? (*Beat.*) How can that be possible?!

Child Voice   Lots of things are possible.

Rory and Child   Any astronaut worth their salt knows that.

2022

McGill   It is four years later.

I can see the grey edges to Sophie's hair. The light catching them. She takes my hand which now I look looks like my mothers. I close my eyes.

'You might not see it now, but this? This is love', she says. 'Something has to move.'

McGill   The sound of the door. When I open my eyes,

I go to the window. The roses.
She's putting bags in the boot of our car. A familiar outline.
She looks up. I duck.
Our car slides out of frame.

I want silence.
But there's the kitchen clock and the fucking tap.
My fucking breathing.
I scrape out a resignation letter.
And I go to work. I have to get a fucking taxi.
I feel nothing. Except maybe a certainty that I have nothing left to give.

Child (*joining the storytelling*)   You didn't know that you were about to meet an astronaut.

McGill   Get back into bed.

Child   I'm just saying, then something did.

McGill   Did what?

Child   Move.

2023

McGill   I get the call in the early hours.

A heart coming from Spain.
Slightly larger than we'd like, but workable the team agrees.

I put my shoes on and go straight in.

I bump into Ellie's mum on the way in. She looks young.
Terrified.

'Tell me it'll be OK. Tell me.'

'I'll be with her all the way through. We can do this.'

'Fuck!' she says.

Washes hands. Holds arms out as though being gowned up.

*Hospital sounds: Have you got / in time for the / the team is ready
for the / if you could prepare the patient then we can get them under
as soon as we /*

The room dims.

*She squeezes her hands closed, then open. Rubs them together slowly.
Warming them up.*

I turn to the small pale chest rising and falling in front of me
as I have time and time again. Take a breath. And I begin.

This is not about death, this story.
My story.
After five hours, I release the clamps.
There are eight seconds of silence . . . eight seconds . . .

(*Four seconds play out.*) . . . before we need the new heart . . .
to beat its way . . . back to life . . . (*Four more seconds.*)

But beat it does. As if saying 'I can. Look I can. I told you. I
can.'

I'm exhausted.

I let myself in the front door.

Instead of turning left into the living room and my chair, I
push against every force and turn my feet up the stairs.

I open the door to our bedroom, mine and Sophie's.
'Please stay,' I hear my voice say to the empty room.

A feeling in my dusty chest.
A flutter and a start.
Beat beat.
Beat beat.
And I reach for the phone to call her.

Slide – child's drawing of a heart

Present

This is not a story about death. It is too enormous. This is about life and love and everything in between.

Child   Look. Your astronaut helmet has a flap and pictures I drew of bumble bees, hearts and moons. It's for if the air gets toxic. It's my old one but done up. Cos I know it works.

McGill   It is the best I've ever seen.

And from me to you . . . (*Thinks quickly.*) . . . Look.

Takes notebook and draws. **Rory** *appears behind her and draws too. She doesn't look at him even when speaking.*

Rory   See? You draw the same person but in a different position on every page. Then flick through the pages and it looks like /

Child   / He's jumping. Boink boink boink . . .

McGill   Rory! What's he doing? Hitting his head on the ceiling?!

Rory   Now, vrooom vroom. Speech bubble, he's saying . . .

Rory *and* **Child**   'So long, grafidyyyyy.'

Rory   Flying jump right off the page.

McGill   It's a great jump. They look so full of . . . Of life. (*Then.*) I hope you had that. Rory. That you didn't just give in. And drop. I hope you felt the air one last time. And flew. I hope you fucking *jumped*.

Rory (*not hearing*)   There you are, Mam. (*Hands her the page.*) Yours. An adventurer to put in your pocket.
(*Goes to leave and then comes back and kisses her.*) Love you.

Present

McGill   Yesterday, Ellie Lewis's mum clicked in her seatbelt, started the engine, and returned her child back to their world, up the A1, her new heart beating strong. And if I listen? And tune everything else out? I can hear his too. And I feel so proud.

Holding a heart in your hands, how does it feel? Like a huge responsibility.
We try to offer quality of days *and* quantity of days. And we're getting better at it. We're getting . . . at helping people to . . . live.
Aren't we?

I have held over a hundred hearts in my hands.
Gifted organs.
Donated. In an incomprehensible act.
Through that tangled net of grief and impotence,
In an absolute act of love.

Which is where you come in. Custodians of that treasure, whichever path you choose.
Look after it. Look after *you*. You can do it.
(*Takes out a crumpled letter.*)
My resignation. I never did hand it in. My job, it's who I am.

We reach for life. You know?
Hanging on as we spin.
It's just that for some, sometimes, we lose our pull.
Or maybe it loses its grip on us.

I'm sorry this has deviated. (*References soggy notes.*) My notes . . .!
The snow. The weather is predictably unpredictable. And I like to walk nowadays.

On my way here tonight, the bells of St Nicholas started to ring.

Peals of them vibrating through my bones, filling every gap.

What an adventure.

Ellie's Voice   Will you know if it has travelled? Or if the person was brave? How can you tell if it's honest? Will it know it's not in the right person? Will I be able to feel it? I mean differently to mine?

Will I still like spaghetti hoops? Baked beans? Marmite?

What if it's been married. Will it like me?

What if it's been to space?!

The bells of St Nicholas ring out.

McGill   I can speak on many things. About facts and formulas, what we can do and what we have yet to progress.

But about this beautiful dangerous thing we hold inside, this pulsing warrier engine? This pump, this furnace, this supposed centre of it all. Hard-working flesh and fibre.

For all my adult 'expertise' . . .

I have to tell you, I still don't know how it all works.

Do you?

End.

fangirl,
or the justification of limerence

Naomi Obeng

Notes on the world of the play

Suggestions for sung parts in **bold**.

When online, the performers do not interact physically, when offline, they can and do. Online has a different texture to offline, it is an emotionally heightened space but avoid garish / loud / circus-like depiction of the internet. It needs to feel natural and unforced. Consider when they are speaking and when they are typing. The distinction between online and offline blurs and breaks down in Scene Five.

Perhaps tell the story like David Lynch would tell it – with simmering horror and a nod toward the incalculable divine.

This is a work of fiction. Any similarity to persons alive or dead, or actual events, is purely coincidental.

Characters

Clara
Chorus One / **Aaron** / **Deb**
Chorus Two / **Ri** / **Emmie**
God, *a famous musician, or rather,* **Clara**'s *idea of him*

'i ain't reading all that
i'm happy for u tho
or sorry that happened'

Scene One

A timeless liminal space which looks vaguely sacred. Altars or vaulted arches. A place of spirituality and worship. **Chorus** *are assembled,* **Clara** *among them.*

Chorus Every day we praise you, God.
You guide us through all weather.
Our anchor in the storm.
The flame that keeps us warm.
You are everlasting, God.
Through thick and thin.
Our reason for living.
You are our Everything.
You show us the path.
You teach us to love.
You are Love.
We'll follow you,
To the end of our days.
With joy in our hearts.
Every day we praise you, God.
This is how it starts.
It's You Forever.
You Forever.

Clara I love Him so much.
I love Him so much I could die.

Chorus Guide us through life's confusion.
Be our connection with perfection!
The constant in life's maelstrom!
Our joyous shining, singing Sun!
The answer to every single motherfucking question!
The hottest musician in Internet Fandom!
It's You Forever. You Forever. You Forever.

'You Forever' refrain crescendos.

Clara *sits cross-legged, staring at her phone.*

Clara   How is he so perfect though?
Literally look at his face.
He's so perfect oh my GOD YOU ARE SO PERFECTTTT
I'M GONNA DIE.

She's so overcome she has to step away from her phone to calm down for a sec. She comes back to her phone.

Clara   And talented.
And beautiful.
And, funny?
You can't sing like a divine being from heaven and URGH
Be hilarious as well?
It's not fair.
Can you not? Please?
It pisses me off!
And he's kind
And his smile
He makes me so happy
How is he so perfect?
Urgh.
Howwww
Whyyyyy

Whimpers.

I could diiiiiiieeeeeeeeeee

Snap.

Suddenly at a train station. Hubbub. **Chorus One** *plays* **Aaron.**

Aaron   Clara! We're going to miss the train. What are you doing?

Clara   Aaron, I can't go now I'm nearly at the front of the queue. The stupid green loading bar's been staring me down for the last ten minutes. (*Whispers into phone.*) I will defeat you.

They say there's wifi on the train . . . but no, there's never wifi on the train. It's not my fault. If you want to blame anyone blame the Tories. And capitalism. And the privatisation of British Rail.

Aaron   Seriously. The train's leaving in two minutes, we have to go.

Clara   No, I'll lose my place and I'll be back at number one billion and it'll be all sold out.

Aaron   You already have three world tour hoodies. You don't need another one. Let's go.

Clara   It's limited edition!

Aaron   It's completely unhinged.

Beat.

Clara   Aaron. It's not just a hoodie. If I get pre-sale merch I'll be on the VIP guestlist for an intimate and exclusive live show in London, where I will be centimetres from God's stupid perfect face. He'll literally reach out his hand toward me during 'You Forever' and I'll stare into his eyes, his actual real life unpixelated eyes, do you understand? And I'll tell him I love him and that is literally all I've ever wanted.

Aaron   That's all you've ever wanted . . .

Clara   Aaron . . .

Chorus Two   Please board the train on platform nine AS IT IS READY TO LEAVE.

Aaron   You spend more time on those dumb fan pages than you do with me.

Clara   It's not that deep. I'll get another train.

Aaron   But I've paid for this one already. Do you even wanna meet my mum? Or did you engineer this so you / didn't have to

Clara   I'm not a criminal mastermind, Aaron, I'm just a simple girl buying limited edition merch.

Chorus Two *blows a whistle.*

Aaron   Two years, and you still haven't met my parents. This isn't what a girlfriend does, Clara.

Clara   Well you don't have some abstract girlfriend, you've got me. I've waited half my life to see him live. Life's disappointing enough, give me this one thing!

Aaron   Well I'm sorry I'm so disappointing . . . My mum's spent all day cooking for us you know. Can you not forget your stupid popstar for one weekend?

Clara (*gasp*)   I'm fifth in the queue!

Aaron   You're not in love. You're obsessed.

He goes to board the train.

Clara   I'm fine. I'll get the next train.

Aaron   Don't bother! Go back to your stupid fanclub.

Clara   Fine. I will. They're fun. They respect me.

World dims. Screen light flickering on her face, drawing her in.

Chorus   It's you Forever. You Forever. You Forever.

Clara   I got the merch
I'm finally going to witness God
In
The
Flesh
I'm calling him God, for legal purposes, by the way, cos this story gets a little.
Complicated.

Scene Two

Online. They don't interact physically.

    Clara   We are wholly unprepared for this spiritual experience, Ri. I will implode.

Ri   I'll hug him so hard his head falls off and he'll be like 'Please put my head back on dear Ri' and I'll be like 'Of course, it would be the pleasure of a lifetime my Short Northern King'.

Clara   CA-CK-LING. THREE SYLLABLES. Please don't decapitate him with your girthy love.

Ri (*enumerating*)   I've had a vision. I will tremble. I will go weak at the knees. I will fall. He will catch me. He will stop the show. He will say 'Ri. Ri. Are you alright?' In his angel voice. And I will say 'Yes. I've seen the light', and I will stroke his soft face with the back of my slowly withering right hand. Then I shall perish.

Clara   Oddly specific.

Clara   WE'RE FINALLY GONNA KNOW WHAT HE SMELLS LIKE

Deb *appears on the thread.*

Deb (*dead serious*)   Hard to describe. Very attractive. Clean. Expensive.

Ri   You're so lucky, Deb. Literally, the idea of you takes up at least half of one of God's brain cells. Swoon.

Deb   Front row at ten concerts over three years on two continents. The kids think their mum's loopy and my husband is a certified saint.

Ri   I wanna be you when I grow up!

Clara   What is this?? They haven't cut to our man in at least ten minutes. Fire the camera operators! You guys watching?

Deb   Kids are asleep. White wine and cheetos at the ready.

Ri   Give God Artist of the Year already!!

Deb   I thought you weren't going to be around, Clara.

Clara   I missed the train to get on the guest list and now my bf's pissed.

Ri   Girl. Respect.

Clara   He doesn't understand. I'd literally do anything to behold this man. He's given me so much.

Ri   That's hot, Clara, surely.

Clara   You'd think. I feel kinda shitty though. Got the baby blue hoodie. First class delivery. I'm gonna wear it at the show.

Ri   Jealous. Blue was sold out for me

Clara   God better win this award, I am here to have a nice time!

Deb   He won't win. Common knowledge, they're are biased against him as a Brit.

They gasp as God appears on their screens. Maybe a flash of beautiful light.

Clara   HE'S SO BEAUTIFUL. I will actually combust. Deb has anyone in the fandom spontaneously combusted before?

Ri   Here we gooooo!

Deb   Ready for the plan if he wins?

Clara   Yes, boss.

Ri   Squeeeeeee

Chorus   Fandom poised, around the world, white-knuckle riding the intermittent loading screens on our dodgy illegal streams, forgetting to breathe, that dimple when He grins (*gasp*)**, heart in my mouth, waiting, bated breath, for the TikTok girlie at the podium to speak the words 'the award goes to . . .'**

Beat.

Clara *screams excitement, celebrations . . .*

Clara   HE'S WON?
HE'S ACTUALLY WON!
The rest of the fandom is equally stoic and restrained:

Beat. Everyone screams, excitement, celebrations . . .

    Clara   Screaming, crying, throwing up.

    Deb   A beautiful speech. Eloquent. Dignified.

    Ri   One sec getting His award reaction face tattooed on
my butt.

    Clara   I have never felt so ALIVE. In. My. Entire.
Existence.

    Ri   That speech was so babygirl, he had me by the
throat I swear.

    Clara   HE'S SO SEXY. HE'S SO FUCKING HOT, RI
KILL ME NOW KING I AM REVELLING.

Clara   We voted and we prayed but
Surely the BTS fans had this one.
They are organised.
And scary.

    Deb   Let the plan begin

Clara   My five fan edit pages are popping off already
Clips of the award win are appearing all over my feeds
We are to unleash a collective onslaught of content
Deb's engineered a strategic and unignorable display of love
and affection
Fans used to plaster posters of musicians on their walls
Now we plaster the internet with shitposts and memes
It's more eco-friendly
And way (all caps) MORE FUN
I'm already extracting video clips of the speech
My role is to unleash the fancams
I'm not saying I'm famous for them but the holy grail of
horny fandom content is a lil video I made, entitled:

    Ri   'God's left wrist for two minutes straight!'

Clara   Three point two million views. Truly unhinged.

   Ri   Your wrist edit is my religion no joke

Clara   Ri's studying to be a doctor you know

   Ri   I think about it every single day I swear

Clara   We will tell our grandkids of this glorious night.
Their grandkids will tell their grandkids – probably via
elaborate tapestries woven by candlelight (after the
inevitable civilisational decline and technological
apocalypse).
I want to get one million views in twenty-four hours on a
new fancam
Maybe I'm delusional but it's totally possible
Though first I must avoid being slain by his beauty in the
process
Cos it's taken me about ten minutes to watch a two minute
video
He's too beautiful
I'm so proud of him

She pauses a video to catch her breath and shake it out.

Clara (*to audience*)   What? You've ever seen someone so
beautiful they make you cry?
Sucks for you.
Our fandom is glorious
We're dancing
We're hugging through our screens
We're side-eyeing Taylor Swift
There's nowhere I'd rather be tonight
Even normies are catching wind of our succulent posts

   Deb   They'll be fully fledged fangirls within a week,
including the straight guys. I've seen it before.

Clara   It's really working
They're liking, they're sharing and our hashtags are
trending!
It's like marketing, except more horny

I AM REVELLING
Not even the trolls can slow me down.

> **Chorus One**   Music for prepubescent hormonal babies
>
> **Clara**   Prepubescent and hormonal? Make it make sense my G
>
> **Chorus Two**   SO SHIT today music makes throw up over fangirl
>
> **Clara**   Hast thou heard of GRAMMAR?
>
> **Chorus One**   Nice to see you're deep in the abuser cult
>
> **Clara**   Not today, BEELZEBUB! Seek help! Find joy! Choose love!
>
> **Chorus Two**   Noah Fence but looking at your account, you just seem like you're ugly
>
> **Clara**   Very creative! Five stars.

Clara   I drop the bomb and click post on my fancam
The title I've picked is:

> **Ri**   'GOD being babygirl at the VMAs for three minutes straight.' Ugh. It's perfect.

They all sort of melt.

Clara   He's so beautiful

I'm so proud of him he's so funny he's amazing
fufckkkkkkfdkdkfkdlfsjlfs

OK

OK.

Composes self. Plays video.

Clara   I know his face by heart it practically feels like my own
When I move my mouth I imagine his
When I smile it's his smile

The fandom subreddit where I'm a moderator is buzzing
like it's never buzzed before
The fun sub mind,
Not the boring one where they're too pious to make fun of
God's bad haircuts
Look, if making fun of your celeb crush by photoshopping
him as various root vegetables isn't love then I don't know
what is
How else would you find out that God looks hot as a yam
We are internet-sphere pioneers
But it's not even just the fandom sharing the content now?

Ri   Normies on twitter are pitching in!

Deb   They'll be fully fledged fangirls within a week

Clara   IT'S THE FIRST FANCAM OF THE SPEECH
PEOPLE LOSE THEIR MINDS
IT'S DOING NUMBERS
I'M LEVITATING
I'VE BEEN STUCK IN ALL CAPS FOR THE LAST FIVE
MINUTES
I DON'T CARE
What if God sees it?
What if he finds me at the London show
And he pulls me in close and whispers 'Clara I saw what you
made'
And I whisper 'Did you like it?'
And he says 'Come backstage'.
And then I marry him
Ahem.
My fancam's already at five-K views. What!
More clips
More memes
More videos

*Dramatic shift of perspective. We see her objectively, in physical
reality. She's sitting alone in the dark laughing into her phone.*

It's weird.

Snap back.

Deb Trending globally on five platforms, team! Keep
sharing the love! Reminder: if you get flagged for spam
log off, and wait twenty minutes before posting again

Clara I've never seen anything like it,
Fans all around the world in their bedrooms in their flats in
their garden sheds, cos obvs they've been relegated by their
jealous spouse (in this economy! choose love!)
10 p.m. Eastern is 1 a.m. here so now the ceremony's over
it's . . .
Later than I'd like to admit.
I forgot to eat tea.
But now even one of my Instagrams is being resurrected
And we all know insta is the Gobi Desert where fan
communities dry up and die
That's why I've only got two accounts there
One isn't even a fandom account, it's so lowkey people
mistake it for God's secret Instagram?
I get the most random DMs from fans sometimes

Ri Hey God, is that you? I love you so much you're my
favourite person in the world I'd do anything for you

Clara Is this what it's like being God-level famous? Sweet.
I have enough edit requests to be here for a week
But I'm nothing if not dedicated to our community
And God
And his tight ass
Which is the next fancam I post. What?
Back to sharing memes with the fervour of a spam bot
One gets a like from GOD'S MANAGER GREGG!

Clara OK, Ri real talk team: do you think if Gregg likes
me it's possible that God might just spontaneously wed
me?

Ri Guys. Have you seen this?

They hit a wall. Silence as they take in streams of new content.
Flickering. Scrolling.

Clara   I don't get it.

Deb   What are they talking about, what allegation?

Ri   The post got deleted. Look, it was this Instagram account.

Clara   Um. What am I looking at? Who's GossipB?

Deb   She calls herself a celeb news site.

Ri   Ten thousand followers on Insta.

Deb   I can't find the post. She's taken it down.

Ri   Someone's reposted it.

Clara   LINK. NOW!

Deb   Why are all these people so angry? What did the post say?

Ri   God slept with a fan.

Pause.

Ri   Assaulted. Is what they're saying. Actually. She said she was eighteen, but she was younger. She said it happened last year.

Clara   Come on. Anyone can post anything. I kissed Kylie Minogue at the BRIT Awards. Post. See! Now you just can't get it out of your head. Doesn't make it true.

Ri   STOP. This is serious.

Clara   It's the internet, Ri, nothing is serious.

Deb   Just ignore it. These accounts invent facts for money. It's all about the clicks.

Clara   Ludicrous. People are, and I cannot stress this enough, idiots. It's stupid. Has God ever been involved in drama?

Deb   Never. The very day he wins a VMA too.

Clara   Maybe the butthurt BTS fans planted it.

Ri   That's not their style.

Clara   Siphoning off our buzz.

Ri   It's all over rumour twitter.

Clara   Why are they sharing it? God is the last person on earth / who

Deb   Don't be alarmed but Gregg texted me.

Ri   Gregg texts her???

Deb   He's a little perturbed.

Clara   I'm fucking perturbed we have to stop this slander!

Deb   He's seen the sub.

Clara   What?

Ri   'The kindest man in the universe who I truly would let use me as a dishrag might really be a predatory piece of shit and I have lost all hope for humanity. Ask me anything'

Clara   See this is why normies think we're insane. I'm closing the thread.

Ri   You can't close it just cos you don't like it. What if it's true.

Clara   Yes I can. I'm admin. It's fake news. God is not a predator.

Deb   Insta-girlie is claiming her 'source' wants to remain 'anonymous'.

Clara   Which is gossip for: this girl doesn't even exist!

Ri   It's like she's come in and pissed all over our sacred space, and then shit in it.

Clara   And now she's charging for entry.

Ri   What?

Clara   She's got a subscriber-only newsletter teasing 'exclusives'. Can people stop monetising every single shred of existence, please.

Ri   I hate this.

Clara   Who does she think she is? Normies will lap this up. They love to tear anyone down. They'll think it's actually true.

Deb   Guys.

Beat.

Deb   There's talk about cancelling the VIP show.

Clara   What? No.

Deb   It's the only event he's got lined up and they're worried about backlash. A fan knows an insider at the label.

Clara   A rumour about a rumour! Bloody hell!

Clara   Nothing's even happened. Literally nothing has happened!

Chorus   It's you Forever. You Forever. You Forever.

Scene Three

Cold stark physical reality.

Clara   I haven't slept.
The sun's coming through the curtains
I sit through the morning scrolling hashtag GOD in a daze
Aaron's decided to spend the weekend at his mum's without me.
He messaged from the train yesterday
I try hard to ignore this as evidence that the train did in fact have wifi.

I only moved into his flat at the start of the year cos it would be cheaper for both of us.

And because I love him, obviously.

My job's a joke and his is zero hours and he wants to be able to save for a pension or whatever

There's nothing edible in the fridge.

I wonder how He sleeps? God.

Does he sleep on his side.

Or on his back? Is he one of those weirdos who sleeps without a pillow?

We can work with that no one's perfect.

Does he curl up?

Is he still up at five like me.

Imagine myself in his arms.

I know Him by heart.

His birthday is seventeenth September he was born at two pm in St. Mary's Hospital when he was eight he moved to Munich which he didn't like his grandmother played him doo-wap records that's how he learned to sing when his mum had cancer he drove two hours each day to see her in hospital and would eat hula hoops from the vending machine to this day hula hoops make him sad his favourite colour is emerald green and he was bullied at school like me. He would never abuse his position. He'd never abuse a fan.

She bites her nails. Bad habit.

Skin. Eyes. Dimple when he smiles. I was so close.

> **Chorus One**   Fan for three years. I am truly disgusted. Merch is going in the trash.

> **Clara**   You clearly aren't a real fan then.

> **Chorus Two**   Always thought he was suspect, too private, something to hide

> **Clara**   Hating because a celeb is 'too private'? Ludicrous.

Chorus One   Let's cancel all celebrities! The entire crop is rotten

Clara   Have some hope for humanity!

Ri   I am ashamed of myself for supporting this man

Clara   Ri?

Ri *looks surprised.*

Ri   What? I've done some digging.

Clara   Don't be ridiculous. Get some sleep.

Ri   I believe women.

Clara   So do I but there's no evidence that the woman in question even exists.

Ri   There's a screenshot of the message the victim sent to GossipB . . .

Clara   This is babygirl God we're talking about. You said you wanted to die in his arms! Thousands of fangirls would leap at the chance to get with him, Ri.

Ri   He assaulted her. Coerced the poor girl.

Clara   Is that what they're saying? Can't you see the whole narrative is whacked? It's like they wrote some bullshit assault story and applied it to whoever was trending. If it was some sleazy indie frontman I'd believe it, but it's God we're talking about Ri. He doesn't even go to afterparties! Any fan knows that.

Ri   He *says* he doesn't go to afterparties.

Clara   Who have you been talking to? They're bloody radicalising you.

Ri   No. I've been doing internet research. He coerced this poor girl.

Clara   You don't even believe what you're saying, do you?

Ri   I don't know. But I don't want to be wrong.

Clara   Let's fight for the VIP show, a group of us are contacting the label. You can sign your name too.

Ri   They say if you side with him you're automatically a misogynist.

Clara   Come on, Ri. Don't you think we'd have heard something? In the five years we've been part of this community? Deb would known something, she basically built the fanclub. He knows her by name! Real fans don't give up on their man before he even gets to speak. I thought we were a team. Have a fucking spine, Ri. Ri? Ri?

Snap. Cold reality, it's night.

Clara   I didn't know there was an angry way to boil miscellaneous pasta but I managed it.
Aaron's ghosting me.
I think I should say sorry but I know he'd make me spell out exactly what I'm sorry for, so I'm quite glad he doesn't pick up actually.
And anyway, the gossip girl's Instagram page is becoming a problem
Pastel colour scheme
Loopy handwritten graphics
Her follow count's gone up by 500 in the last ten minutes
I know this because I have been watching her follow count go up for the last ten minutes
Her latest pinned post:

'Guys, the God situation is obviously delicate legally but trust me it'll all come out and you're not ready for it. Be sure to sign up to my exclusive subscription-only newsletter to get the latest updates.'

The more I stare at her posts
The more sleek and cool she seems
The more I hate her.
Sitting there in her anonymity.

Profiting off curated lies.
I know the rumour's gone mainstream cos randos who know
absolutely nothing are claiming to know absolutely
everything incredibly loudly

>**Chorus Two**   I heard he has a dungeon in his house it's
>in the council planning records, Google it

>**Chorus One**   The label's known for years but they NDA
>the women so it never comes out. She's so brave.

>**Chorus Two**   I know it's true cos she's a friend of a
>friend I went to high school with and the whole school
>knows he gave her chlamydia FACT

Clara   She even has merch! A gossip site!
There she is, lapping it up and pissing me off!

>'I always say this guys. Fans are so weird. Celebs are just
>people OK. People suck. Like, do you worship people with
>normal jobs? Doctors? People who contribute to society.'

>**Clara**   GOD DOES CONTRIBUTE TO SOCIETY.

Clara   Like selling out a stadium tour is worthless
Like creating moments of pure bliss
Allowing ordinary people to transcend the dullness and
worry of daily existence for two hours and find JOY
So much so that they'll travel across the world to experience
it again and again
Like that isn't contributing to society?

>**Clara**   YOU'RE PATHETIC. YOUR ACCOUNT IS
>EMBARRASSING. GOD HAS DONE NOTHING
>WRONG AND YOU KNOW IT. HOW DARE YOU.
>TAKE BACK THE ALLEGATION AND FUCK OFF!

We wait, sit in it til the lack of response irks her.

>**Clara**   He cares about his fans! He'd never take
>advantage of ANY of us.

Chorus One   IDK sixty pounds for a hoodie? That's abusive

Clara   YOU'RE IGNORING MY COMMENTS COS YOU KNOW YOU'RE WRONG. I WON'T STOP. ALL YOU CARE ABOUT IS ATTENTION NOT TRUTH. YOU DISGUST ME. GOD IS INNOCENT. YOU PICKED THE WRONG FANS TO MESS WITH. WE'RE NOT LETTING YOU GET AWAY WITH THIS. ANSWER ME COWARD. I THOUGHT YOU CRAVED ATTENTION. WELL NOW YOU'RE GETTING IT.

Clara   DUMB BITCH

Clara   LIAR! I HOPE YOU BURN IN HELL

Clara   She's typing.

Beat.

Chorus Two   Aw. Babe. Your man's finished. Have a good life, if you ever get one.

Clara   DON'T YOU F -

Clara   She blocked me.

Pause.

I still have my second Insta, though. Why would I let her win?

An angrier tempo finds **Clara** *and* **Chorus** *back in prayer, prayer becoming more of a rallying cry.*

Clara   Our guide through life's confusion. Our connection with perfection. Our reason for living. Our one constant in life's maelstrom. Our joyous shining, singing Sun.

Chorus *and* **Clara   It's You Forever. You Forever. You Forever.**

Scene Four

Stark physical reality. A grey morning.

Clara   Monday morning. Only managed two misshapen
hours' sleep.
I'm going be late so I email in sick for work, describing in
vivid detail how much I've puked.
I have a message from Deb saying she's been crying at her
kitchen table
The BurnGod and GodIsAnAbuser campaigns are getting
nasty

> **Deb**   It's not fair. He's the kindest, funniest, most giving
> man. He radiates love as soon as you meet Him. And
> now all these anon accounts attacking me for loving
> him?

Clara   I told them I just wanted to know who she was
Behind the pastel and DM screenshots
The fans on the boring sub
Have certain skills
Obtaining information through not entirely legal means
They're actually not that bad when you talk to them
They only want the best for God
They're the only ones left with their heads screwed on
We dig in the digital dirt
Doesn't take too long
To find her personal account.
Detached air of superiority in the bio
It's definitely her
Her name is Emma.
Emmie.
One of the sub stans asks what I'm going to do now
God changed my life.
His songs are like they're speaking just to me.
I can save him if no other fans have the guts.
Take down the Death Star, and blow up the whole Empire.

She sits up.

Clara But I've got a message from Emmie already. Two years ago. June.

Emmie Hey, I don't know if this is actually you . . . God?

Clara *takes in the turn of events, gleefully. Then catches herself.*

Emmie You changed my life. Your lyrics speak to me, it's like they're written for me. I know you didn't make this account for fans to find haha, but thank you for everything you do. Would love to talk some time. Love and admiration, Emmie.

Beat.

Clara Cringe.

Pause.

Clara If I can't have the encounter with God I dreamt of, then maybe she can. I know him by heart.

Clara Hi Emmie. It's God.

We wait. Spotlight on **Chorus Two***, who now plays* **Emmie***.*

Emmie Wow. What? Oh my god.

Clara Apologies.

Clara God would definitely say 'apologies'.

Emmie Oh my god don't apologise!

Clara This is weird for me too.

Pause.

Emmie Is this a prank?

Clara This isn't a prank. You're talking to God.

Pause.

Emmie Actual God. In my DMs.

Clara God who's about to get screwed.

Emmie   Oh. You know who I am then?

Beat. **Clara** *bites her nails.*

Emmie   How did you find this account?

Clara   I have my sources. Your anonymous 'victim' seems to want to play both sides.

Emmie   Interesting.

Beat.

Clara   I'm not here to mess around. Take the posts down. Tell your followers it was a lie.

Emmie   I trust my source.

Clara   And if my lawyers were involved? That won't end well for you.

Emmie   Are you threatening me?

Clara   Am I threatening her?

Emmie   My source wouldn't lie. Why would she lie? She's a victim.

Clara   You went out of your way to find my secret account and DM me professing your love . . . People do all kinds of crazy things.

Emmie   That's normal. I was a fan.

Clara   Was?

Beat.

Emmie   I admit it's a thrill when celebs reach out. You're pretty charming even through a screen.

Clara   It's been said.

Clara   OK she's insane. SHE'S AN INSANE PERSON. She's loving this. She wants the attention. She wants the celebs begging her for mercy in the DMs.

Emmie   It's not why I do it though. I sat on that message for months. I didn't wanna believe it. It hurt to read.

Clara   You're going to ruin my life. Do you enjoy that?

Emmie   No. I don't want to do that.

Clara   Then don't. Please, Emmie. You seem like a reasonable person.

Emmie   I'm not a journalist. It's not always 100 per cent accurate info. My account is entertainment. It's a distraction. It's for fun.

Clara   Must be very normal, wanting to ruin my career for fun. You know I'm a real person right?

Emmie   Yes . . .

Clara   I've never even met the girl. My fans know that. That's why they're supporting me.

Emmie   A lot of them are taking her side. Actually.

Clara   I could tell everyone who you are. I'm sure the stans would have fun doxxing you and your family into oblivion.

Beat.

Emmie   Wow. You really are a piece of shit.

Clara   You'll be hearing from my lawyers!

Emmie   Your fans have no idea who you are. Do they? If they did they would hate you. I run my account to keep fans safe from people like you.

Clara   She's sent a screenshot of a message. It's long. And a private exchange between God and the anonymous woman, it looks real. I don't think she should have sent it to me. It feels too. Intimate. She spent so long not wanting to see herself as a victim but she realised she had to tell someone. I scan through it, but even scanning I feel her hurting.

Emmie   She thought she loved you. Don't you spend hundreds of thousands on making sure that they have every reason to?

Clara   It's all lies! You don't know Him.

Clara   Shit.

Emmie   Who? Oh. You really thought I'd believe I was talking to God. Nice try.

Clara   You believed it! You were loving it! You just can't stop lying can you? You will have nothing left by the end of this. We'll fight for him. We won't let you win!

Beat.

Emmie   Seek help. I'm exposing you. Screenshots are going in my stories tomorrow. Stans need to learn about consequences. Blocked. Reported.

Clara   I'm exhausted but that doesn't mean I don't believe what I see, cos suddenly, there's light in the flat and the ceiling unfolds, a throne, high in the heavens, the silhouette of a man, and around his waist a crescent of pale bluebirds fluttering for freedom, a terrible light pierces his chest, a search beam sweeping down trawling the blackened earth. I see now he's on fire, desperate, flames kiss his knees and bubbling black soot falls as he calls out, His angel voice of Heaven unmistakable, my name, he's saying, as the search beam falls on my frame and flames creep up him, blistering. All our dancing, posting, willing his almighty ascent back into the light does nothing. It's not enough. He is burning, flickering, falling. Soon he'll be only a word spoken in whispers by those who never stopped believing. He reaches down his hand toward me, and summons me, by his Grace, to levitate, to shine, send him ascending again. He's urging me to see the shape of his Glory, as the others fall and writhe blindly in the corrupted soil.

**God   You have Faith while others are scared to believe
anything at all. Have faith. It's You Forever. You
Forever.**

Snap.

Clara   I'm sitting on the only sliver of bench that's free of
bird shit
I wasn't aware that there was an angry way to ingest food
truck chips but, I found one.
I still feel empty
Aaron's calling again
(*Answering the phone.*) What?

We watch her emotions change as she listens to **Aaron***. He wants to
break up. He's seen what she's been posting online. He feels like he
doesn't know her. He wants her to move out of his flat.*

Clara   Please don't call me that.
Please.

He hangs up.

Clara *speaks to the* **Chorus** *now.*

Clara   He wants me out of the flat before he gets back
tomorrow.
Your heart's not a cake, is it?
You can give it all to someone and still have it all to give.

The **Chorus** *comfort her.*

Clara   What does the headline say?

Chorus   Singer charged with sexual assault

**Chorus   You are everlasting, God.
Through thick and thin.
Our reason for living.
Our Everything.
It's You Forever.
You Forever. You Forever. You Forever. You Forever. You
Forever.**

Scene Five

'You Forever' loops and morphs into a darker, more nightmarish tune, a kind of sick beat that carries **Clara** *along for the next scene.*

The online voices bleed into physical reality for the first time.

Chorus Two   You're an abuser just like Him, go touch grass. Preferably forever.

Chorus One   SO glad they exposed her. We fucking hate you Clara.

Clara   I put my phone on airplane mode and watch the fields trundle by.
When I'm finally home at my parents' house I sink my face into a bowl of leftovers and practically inhale them.
Glimpse myself in the mirror,
Not a fallen angel, no.
I remember when God got a new girlfriend, the fandom went feral, some Brigitte Bardot babe, stunning, but she was just a reminder that God was never into girls who looked like me
I was nineteen years old the first time a guy told me I was beautiful
Is that sad? I've never admitted that to anyone.
It took me by surprise
To be desired. Aaron desiring me.
He called me heartless on the phone.
Said I didn't know how to love.
I'm scared he might be right.
Dear God, how do I know how I'm meant to feel?

Scene Six

Clara *knocks on the door of* **Aaron**'s *flat, wiping away tears before he sees her.*

Clara   I know you don't want to see me.

Aaron   I was asleep, ideally I wouldn't be seeing anyone . . . I thought you'd gone home. Gone offline. That was good for you.

Clara   You were right. And I'm sorry.

Beat.

Aaron   And what exactly are you sorry for?

Pause.

Clara   I don't know.

Aaron   Clara.

Clara   I don't know.

Aaron   You came all the way here to tell me you're sorry about 'you don't know'? I'm going back to bed.

Clara   Well I only came to get my things actually. I couldn't move everything out myself last week. You didn't give me much time /

Aaron *dumps two plastic bags of her things in front of her.*

Clara   Thanks. I got fired by the way.

Aaron   You hated that job.

Clara   I did. You always knew me better than I knew myself.

Beat.

Did you tell your mum why I didn't come?

Aaron   Did I tell my mum that my girlfriend thought buying merch was more important than building a future together? I should have. I should have said that, yes. But sometimes, you keep the truth to yourself, to avoid causing someone else pain.

Clara   I don't love you anymore. I'm sorry.

Aaron   I still love you. But that's OK.

Pause.

Uh. This came too. I opened it by accident. Assumed it was for me.

He hands her a torn open package. **Clara** *takes the package. Pulls out the sleeve, a baby blue hoodie.*

Clara   Oh.

She holds the package awkwardly.

Aaron   Was it worth it? Cos I never understood, Clara. I thought you'd get over him. Grow out of it. I'm upset when Liverpool lose, but I don't let it ruin me.

Clara   I don't think we have feelings because they're worth it?

Aaron   You're right there. Spot on.

He goes to leave.

Clara   I'm sorry for not giving you time. And I'm sorry I don't always know what I should be sorry for.

Beat.

Clara   I love the escape of it. Getting away from the . . . enshittening of everything. I love the image. I love the image and the idea and the desire and the longing and emotion and the community and the myth-making, the excitement, and the jokes and the glee and the shitposts and the glorious all encompassing unknown and the unattainable perfection. I love fantasising and sinking in and letting go and hoping. Dreaming out of this terrible world full of death and corruption and dead-ends and cruelty and mediocrity and having to settle for less because the system's built to make it so impossible to have more, I love dreaming out of all that into joy. Actual real, simple joy. I love imagining. I love the comfort of longing. I fucking love the longing and forgetting myself. Having purpose. Giving myself fully with no filter. The slipping into simplicity and knowing that I can feel all that without having to see myself through someone else's eyes. I love imagining it. It's safer than real love, Aaron. That's why.

After a moment.
They soften.
They hug.
As friends.

Scene Seven

In this embrace, **Chorus One** *ceases to be* **Aaron** *and they are back in the liminal space of the start of the play.*

Chorus   She goes back home. She cries herself to sleep. She spends four months in her childhood bedroom eating crisps, applying for jobs without getting an interview /

Clara   Yeah alright, we get it.

House lights.

Chorus Two *removes the hoodie from the packaging.* **Chorus** *help* **Clara** *to put it on. She stands at the centre, arms outstretched, hood up, anointed, and tired. And embarrassed.*

Chorus One   Don't worry, it'll be vintage soon.

Clara   Are they still talking about me online?

Chorus One   'On the internet no one knows you're a certified psycho. She was out there pretending to BE GOD. full on delulu.'

Clara   I saw a video once about how people my age aren't good at understanding regret?
From birth all we've known is being stuck in looming disasters with no end in sight
We never saw narratives of overcoming the bad cos the bad's still here
We just were taught to accept the being powerless to change it

And we didn't even build the digital world
We weren't even born when they created it
And then we're belittled for living online?
When it's the only space to be with your friends that doesn't
cost money
The only way to escape the narrowing options of reality
I think both online and off look the same to me:
A loveless space where it's way easier to hate than be happy.

Chorus One   Your mistake wasn't loving Him.

Clara *pulls uncomfortably at the hoodie. And takes it off.*

Chorus Two   Let's have some joy here too then. Can we?
Put on a tune. Go on. I dare you.

Clara   Not 'You Forever' please. Makes me cry now. Wait.
Have you heard of this guy?

She shows her phone.

Clara   Also he's pretty cute, not gonna lie.

Chorus One   Incorrigible.

Clara   I'm joking. I'm not. I am. Maybe.

Music. They make space for a new beginning.

End.

with the love of neither god nor state

Vici Wreford-Sinnott

Cast

Greta, early-twenties, loves music, has been brought up in the care system and has a neurodivergent condition. She sometimes speaks in rhymes and rhythm. She fiddles with a friendship bracelet on her wrist on and off throughout the piece. Please see the writer's note below about playing this character.

Thea, mid-fifties, Northern community matriarch who has been part of Northvale Social Club for many years.

Jan, Greta's social worker.

Kia, we only ever meet Greta's friend Kia via text in snapchat but never in person.

Setting

Northvale is a fictional urban community on the edges of the West End of Newcastle. Along the Scotswood Road, under two bridges and beyond, into the shadows near Denton. It has its own local facilities – precinct, takeaways, corner shops, churches, social clubs, and social services.

Writer's notes for director and actor

There is a long history of myths and misrepresentations of disabled characters in theatre and my work is about challenging stereotypes and presenting characters with agency. The character of Greta must be played by a neurodivergent actor with an understanding from direct personal experience of Greta's rhythms of speech and movement, mannerisms, directness of tone in conversation, and stimming. It is imperative that the actor does not feel they have to mimic neurodivergent characteristics and the character must not be played into stereotypes of neurodivergence. As neurodivergent people we can be blunt, matter of fact, and think of our own experience first. We often do, or we often are expected to, mask our real condition and its symptoms. I think it's important that a neurodivergent actor playing Greta is someone who is aware of this in themselves. Gentle stimming as a characteristic of Greta is not to be over emphasised but something as simple as the repetitions and rhythms in speech occasionally and playing with the bracelet from Kia for comfort are good things for the actor to be aware of.

Neurodivergence comes under the umbrella of disability and therefore both director and actor must have a working and lived knowledge of the social model of disability. Greta is not a tragic figure and being disabled does not define her. The way society is organised, the preconceptions of disability and the barriers she has and continues to experience have defined her social status to date. The moment of the play is a pivotal turning point in her life and how she perceives herself in the world. Performing Greta should not be sentimental, tragic or mawkishly emotional.

Writer's note on music

The music must not create feelings of sentimentality or conjure self pity/pity. The lyrics are not 'songs' as such but are part of the dialogue. At the time of publication the music has not been composed and a collaborative process is due to take place but I imagine the lyrics to be somewhat discordant to the music. Ideas for sections to be sung are indented throughout the text. The music and singing must meet the access requirements of neurodivergent people, people with mental health conditions, and Deaf/hearing impaired people.

Wellbeing

When presenting work by people who are marginalised I would advocate that wellbeing support is to be in place for the rehearsal and performance period. Wellbeing should be discussed with the performers in advance as performing elements of our realities, albeit in fictionalised forms, can have an impact on individuals. Hopefully the power of creating work which speaks to the world in important ways will support unity and solidarity amongst the company making it.

One – Tonight

Thea is standing on stage at Northvale Social Club speaking to the audience with a microphone. It's a fundraising evening. Northvale is closing and will become a foodbank and community café full time.

Thea Right everyone, settle down, settle down, let's get started. I knew we weren't going to be ready on time – Big Garry – pass those salt and pepper pots around, come on, get the tables set. Muck in lad **(Thea gestures to people to help pass things around.)** So, welcome folks, comrades, dearly beloved, one and all. As you all know by now Northvale is closing its doors as a social club for the last time tonight, which is very sad when you think of the history these walls hold. The funny little world of this Club has been here for over seventy years, serving local people. Friends and neighbours. We gave it a bloody good go, but here we are, things change and what people need changes. **(Thea begins to sing, ironic cabaret tone.)**

> It's not the sort of place
> That's wanted anymore
> People sit at home now
> And have cans by the telly.
> After wrangling with the committee
> I want to thank you all,
> Even you Johnny Stanger
> you stubborn old bugger.
> Tomorrow the doors open
> renewed purpose and
> new people.
> Sitting bravely here
> In the shadow of that steeple
> The council couldn't give a shit
> So communities have to do our bit.

Tomorrow we become a full time food bank serving hot food to those that need it. So this fundraiser will help get us off to a good start, and you being here means a lot, it really does. We have to look after each other. And no, Big Garry, there isn't a meat raffle tonight – who can even afford to cook meat these days? We are going to be serving you something a little bit special later though.

Two – Last Night

Greta is walking from Elswick to Northvale near Denton, about an hour's walk, when her phone pings. She looks at her phone and reads a Snapchat from friend Kia.

Greta   Greta where R U?

Greta   Walking, walking, walking.

> Tracing the river from Elswick
> Along the Scotswood Road
> Under the two bridges
> And beyond,
> The woman at the precinct
> Said to head for the steeple.
> There's a weird glow,
> Maybe they've got
> one of those light up grottos.
> Mary the chaste, Mary the pure,
> Mary the little waxen statue,
> tears rolling down her face.
> People gathering, clutching their
> plastic cure-all Mary-shaped bottles,
> Cheap as chips Holy Water for sale
> Gawping, prodding, judging.

> I've had enough of people
> Just like Mary I'm sure,
> Enough of people
> making promises they will not keep,
> Of shutting doors on you.
> The straw has broken the camel's back
> It's time for answers.

Greta's phone pings. Greta reads Kia's Snapchat.

Greta   I'm so, so sorry that I had to say you couldn't come round. It's Mum's new boyfriend. I tried. x

It's dark.
No one I know here.
Craggy metal ghosts of industry
Cast shadows even in the dark.
I am Greta Stone, twenty-one years old, have never been out on my own at night.
Normally I am somewhere, not nowhere.

Greta's phone pings. Greta reads Kia's Snapchat.

Greta   Give me the address and I'll try come see U 2morrow.

Kia was my first ever best friend, at the home. 'I love you just as you are' she said. The home took us all to the cinema and I didn't like the dark and the loud, loud sound. She held my hand and kissed it. I wanted to explode from inside out and I ended up standing up and shouting 'atypical sex for atypical people' at a really quiet part. We ran out, 'I can't breathe' she had squawked. 'I'm dying', she said as we both fell on the floor. Best friends. (**Half beat.**) Until she got fostered. She couldn't keep in touch much after that. New family. New life.

> Walking walking walking.
> Hello bushes, hello gate, hello pavement, hello feet, hello wall,
> Goodbye to the river behind me,
> Keep going, keep moving.
> Sometimes the rules don't make sense at all.

I thought I could do it, I did.

And now I don't.
How could I ever do it on my own.
The holy water didn't ever work
The home would take us on trips.

> Make a wish, say a prayer,
> Broken body to repair,
> Cleanse my sins, spare my soul,
> make me well, make me whole.

It's time for answers. I had decided.

And now I'm here
Northvale Social Club
Redbricks with sandstone corners
Crackled in old cream paint.
I try the door.
Of course the door is locked.
Fuck fuck fuck.
I knock.
I knock again.
Open up. Open up.
Every door is locked.
From the wrong side.

My heart. My heart is beating, bursting, thump thump thump.
(**Knocks loudly.**)

Three – Late Last Night

The door swings open. Thea stands furious in the doorway.

Thea   What the hell is all this noise? Can you not read the sign?

Greta (takes deep breaths and takes a well-worn laminated ID card out of her bag)   I am Greta Stone and I am twenty-one years old. This card tells you all about me. I live at the Magpie's Nest Residential Home for Young People, under two bridges down the river that way. I have been in care since I was two. I have never run away anywhere in my life and have always followed the rules. I didn't see the sign.

Thea (looks for the sign but it has gone)   Some little shite-hawk has taken it again. It says to quietly use the side door and think of our neighbours. We're not open until tomorrow.

Greta   I am looking for my family and I am usually somewhere not nowhere.

Thea   Well, they're not here, love, it's just me, and I am very busy.

Greta   A woman, who smelled of chips, told me that you have a heart of gold and told me to follow the steeple and there was a glow and I followed it all the way here. Do you have a heart of gold?

Thea   Have you been taking something?

Greta   No but I am very hungry, I didn't eat at my teatime, can you feed me?

Thea   Are you high, love, you know (**Mimes smoking weed.**)

Greta   I'm not sure what that means.

Thea   You just sound a little bit weird to me.

Greta   I am Greta Stone and I am twenty-one years old.

Thea   Yes, yes love you've told me that bit. I get it.

Greta   There is information on this card about me. What to do if I'm lost, who contact if I'm ill or in case I panic. I have an invisible condition. I have to show my card to you, so that you know what to do.

Thea   So that I know what to do? What that tells me, love, is that I'm not qualified at all. Should you be at the hospital if you're not well?

Greta   No, that's only for when you are ill, and I am obviously not ill.

Thea   Well, it means there's something not right.

Greta (looking over Thea's shoulder)   Where are all the others?

Thea   What others?

Greta   Ones like me who need your help. Like the woman at the precinct said, 'You will do anything for anyone'.

Thea   I think she's jumping the gun a bit there.

Greta   So you don't help people, not if they're people like me? Why do you need a sign that says to come to the side door then?

Thea   Well, as I said, we're not officially open until tomorrow. Look people will be welcome then but I don't have any special skills.

Greta   Walking walking walking. Well, my feet have brought me here for a reason. I thought the glowing lights I could see from the distance were from the church yard, like a little grotto or something. A sign.

Thea   Look, are you sure you're not on something? I can't be having any more trouble round here. They're trying to close me down as it is.

Greta   No little grottos then, like the ones where they give you holy water.

Thea   Nope. No grottos here. No holy water. I think the lights you could see are from the kebab shop. I'm definitely not qualified, love.

Greta   Not qualified for what?

Thea   You know, I'm not able to . . .

Greta   What?

Thea   . . . do what you need.

Greta   What do you think I need?

Thea   I don't know but I don't have any training.

Greta   You don't need training to talk to a person.

Thea   But you said you were, you know . . .

Greta   Yes, My name is Greta Stone. I am twenty-one years old. I have never been anywhere on my own before. The card tells you what to do.

Thea looks at the card.

Greta   I'm just a person, I'm looking for answers and maybe my family. And somewhere to sit down for a while. Do you have a chair?

Thea   We do (**Gestures to chair.**)

Greta   See, (**Sits down.**) no specialist equipment needed.

Thea   No, of course. Here, have some bread (**Thea begins to butter some bread.**)

Greta   Is there nothing hot?

Thea   Not at this time of night, now do you want some bread and butter or not?

Greta (snatches the bread; to audience)   I chitter and chatter and
I start to get around her. Once inside I calm down. I am not on my own
anymore and this is someone who is in charge of things. Someone
else is in charge of the situation, thank god. I think I'm going to burst –

(To Thea, spluttering while eating bread.) I thought I could do it, I
did.

And now I don't. It was a ridiculous idea. How could I ever do it on my
own? It was never going to be allowed.

Thea   Steady, what wasn't going to be allowed?

Four – Earlier Yesterday

Greta

My social worker Jan,
took me to see a flat yesterday.
The view out of the window
Is right up my street.
an estate full of homes,
where lots of families live.
Goes on for miles
Over the horizon.
Opposite is an identical block of flats
and beside it rows and rows
of little box houses.
And they are beautiful.
Beautiful to me.

She's busy with her clipboard when I notice the door.
Four different locks.
First a silver Yale latch.
Next is Chubb lock, old school
I imagine key turning in my hand,
a little bit of resistance and **(Gestures it working.)**
The people before
put a bolt top of the door.
And then, halfway down,
just like on the telly,
a sliding safety chain.

Never before have a series of locks symbolised
so much freedom.

And then Jan's phone rings,
Someone else says it's not to be
Someone else says it's not to be
Someone else says it's not to be.

Five – Late Last Night

Thea   Okay, okay. It's very late. You can stay for one night but ring them and tell them you are safe at least so they are not worrying about you – they'll have half the city out looking for you. You'd better not cause me any trouble.

Greta   I nod. I look at my phone and see the battery has died.

I didn't pack my charger in my back pack of essential and useful things.

I am already not good at survival.

Greta has her back pack and gets her toothbrush out.

Greta
She is cautious about me,
Side eyes me up and down,
She says she's really worried
about getting into trouble.
Makes me sleep in the Church Hall
On the camp bed from the war,
Dark green prickly material,
the smell of all who've lain there before.
The kind where hinges squeak
And elbows creak.
Nowhere is your own.

Thea   Come on, time for sleep. I have a big day tomorrow.

Six – This Morning

Thea (on the phone)   Yes, yes, we are ploughing on. You might have processes at your end but we have people living real lives at this end, hungry. Listen, why don't you come to the fundraiser? Forcing your hand? No, no, no, I just thought you might like to do your bit for the community. You live local don't you, I remember your mam? Busy, ah that's a shame. So, we can go ahead then, yes?

Sounds of people in a busy kitchen, Thea seems stressed and rushed off her feet, moving pans and piles of plates. Raffle tickets. Bunting. A bulb needs changing in the Northvale Club stage sign. Greta appears.

Thea (shouts to the kitchen)   Keep an eye on those loaves in the oven. Tap them on the bottom to check if they are done. (**To Greta.**) Oh, you're still here? I didn't think you'd last the /

Greta   But today is Friday – a very big day at the club. We have to help the community don't we? You need my help.

Thea   In the nicest possible way, I need to plough on with as little distraction as possible.

Greta   I have been looking at all the photographs and all the empty frames.

Thea   Lots of people have never been in this club, felt excluded, and I want to slowly fill those frames up with new people.

Greta   And I was looking at your fliers about the fundraiser, it feels like disabled people are at the very bottom of everyone's list.

Thea   I don't think that's true.

Greta   Where is the word disabled on any of them?

Thea   We don't want to embarrass anyone.

Greta   Why would we be embarrassed?

Thea   It's not a nice thing to be described as, is it? Disabled, like there's something wrong with you.

Greta   I suppose it depends what you think being disabled is.

Thea   You're just being sensitive now. It's clear that everyone is welcome. Now, come on, no more questions. Let me get on.

Greta   I don't think it is clear. I wouldn't know I could come.

Thea   Well, you're here though aren't you.

Look make yourself useful and peel some potatoes. Sit there where I can keep an eye on you.

Thea is visible on the phone, gesturing towards Greta and looking serious. Greta is looking suspiciously at the potatoes.

LOVE SOUP

Thea (hands Greta chopping board and knife and potatoes)
Just peel them. We'll get some soup bubbling before you can say brick shithouse.

Greta   What are we making?

Thea   Soup.

Greta   What kind of soup. I don't like parsnips.

Thea

Love Soup. I serve it at big events and people can't get enough of it.
My mother taught me and my brother how to make it.
Everyone adds a little something,
Chooses it carefully,
prepares it and then
throws it into the pot.
And it all cooks together,
As you talk and laugh.
She taught us that the making
of the soup is a communal task.
Everyone together.
Adding something, changing the flavour.
Everyone's ingredients count.

(Chopping and mixing.)

Greta   Chop, chop, chop, chop,
You have to help out at The Magpie.
Friday. They will be having fish fingers, chips and peas.
Kids food.

Thea   Let's get this boiling.

Greta   Will it take long I'm starving.

Thea   It will take as long as it takes, it's Love Soup
There's no rules.

Greta   You say that as if it is a good thing.
Rules are useful. You shouldn't break rules, it messes things up.

Thea   Rules are made to be broken.

Greta   Not where I'm from.

Thea   What, the home?

Greta   I do want to do the right thing, but I just don't know what that
is anymore.
I've always played by the rules,
Don't rock the boat.
That's what we've always been told,
Whispered to us as a kindness by some care worker,
Don't rock the boat.
Smile and say thank you.

Thea   That's someone who doesn't want the boat rocking for them.

Seven – Sometimes and Always

**There is a whirl of getting ready to impress visitors. Clothes,
face, hair, practising to smile, Greta waves a table cloth as a
top in front of her and arranges vegetable baskets for the raffle
at Northvale and plays with and adds big ribbon bows.**

Greta

Today is 'Everybody Smile Day' at the Magpie
Well-meaning people can be the most dangerous of all

Visitors are coming from all parts of the city
Someone may be getting fostered
Not me.
Jan is kind to me as she knows
how I'll be feeling.
She still gets me ready cos 'you never know'.
Smile and say thank you.

Put on your nicest top.
I ironed it specially.
Want you feeling nice
It will help you to smile.

It's a big day for the home, a great big performance,
Appealing to nice people, to make a good impression.
They're always very eager, trying to be cool,
Clean fingernails and sad eyes,
Today will change their lives.
Smile and say thank you.

Well-meaning people can be the most dangerous of all,
It's hard to be quiet when you're trying to be heard.

I spent my whole life following rules so I was fosterable – so people would like me. It's called masking, you know like hiding who you are and the things you really need from the world to make it work properly.

Eight – Lunchtime Today

Greta and Thea are arranging vegetables for the raffle / peeling vegetables for more soup.

Thea hands Greta her phone. She switches on her phone and messages ping in.

Greta   Kia's been in touch again. (**Reads Kia's message.**) R U at home? What home? I don't have a home. (**Reads next part of Kia's message.**) Look I'm still wearing my bracelet. We made each other friendship bracelets.

Pause.

Greta (phone pings)   I have had a text from my social worker. She says she will see me later?

Thea   I had to let them know you were safe.

Greta   You called them? I don't want them to know where I am.

Thea   I can't risk getting into any trouble about you being here, for me or for Northvale.

Greta   Why would there be trouble? I am an adult. It wasn't time to call them.

Thea   They would have called the police, thought something had happened to you. It sounds to me like you've never been anywhere except that home before and /

Greta   I was once with my family.

Thea   Yes, well, that was different. That was in the past. Look, the social services will know what's best for you.

Greta   Why do people think that? They know nothing about me. I have had to bottle myself inside the whole time I've been there. Smile and say thank you.

Thea   I just mean for your safety.

Greta   No. I would just have to put myself back inside and seal myself in. I have never felt so free as I have the last two days.

Thea   I'm sorry, love.

Greta   Not that face with those eyes, not from you as well. I don't understand you. You talk about helping out local people, about being a community and how come some people are second class in that.

Thea   What do you mean?

Greta   The way you think of me – I'm different, I'm special, I need to be at arm's length cos I need looking after.

Thea   You need proper looking after.

Greta   How do you know what I need?

Thea   You carry a card that tells people.

Greta   That was written by other people, not me. They are not my words.

Thea   Well, it's just that you kept sharing it.

Greta   Maybe it's all I have. Maybe this is who I was told I was.

Thea   We're not geared up to look after people in that way, people with special needs.

Greta   You keep saying that, 'not trained', 'not qualified', 'special needs' – we hate that phrase – do you know that?

Thea   We are talking about you going back to the home so that they can help you get sorted out.

Greta   Oh, we all just need sorting out, don't we – some one else making all the decisions.

Thea   Well, I can't be that, and so you need proper help.

Greta   No. I don't. I need space and someone to speak to me like an adult.

Thea   Well, that's not my job. And so I'm sorry, yes, I did contact the council to let them know you were here and that you were safe. And that they would need to come and get you.

Greta   Why? Why would you do that to me?

Thea   Look, I've got a lot on and I can't let people down.

Greta   Oh, can you not? But you can let me down.

Thea   No, lots of people are depending on me.

Greta   I'm here now and I'm depending on you.

Beat.

We made Love Soup.

Nine – Last Night

Greta   Thea let me charge my phone in her office. I go in there, nobody's supposed to, any of the helpers, as it's just for official business. I look at the pictures on the wall, postcards from club members, and photos of Thea on holiday. There is a black and white photo of a man holding a baby. His face is trying to smile but his eyes show a deep, deep, pain. There are creases on the photo where it's been handled. I hear Thea coming.

Ten – Tonight

Thea (addressing the audience on the microphone: points as if to one of the helpers)   Put some of those forms out on the tables – you need to sign up to something tonight. It's not just about feeling good about yourselves. Do something. I want to thank the mams who have made this food bank and café happen, to fill all those little empty bellies. I cannot bear the thought of hungry children – when did we start accepting that? The people at the top are fucking evil – just in it for themselves and their rich mates, taking more and more from us, and giving more and more to them. It's obscene, man, they don't care if we live or die. Why can people not see it? Where is the outrage? We need to remember who we are. That we come from good people. We're not the mass mess of our own making they say we are. I don't think the gap has ever been wider, not in my lifetime. And they've done it on purpose mind – they know exactly what they are doing, turning us against each other, making us struggle so that we cannot bloody think straight. Anyway – here's to the mams, the matriarchs, the sisters who have pulled together. Come on, dig deep, everyone you meet is having a hard time. Do what you know is right – take action, speak out, even when those bastards in London are trying to silence us with all their new laws. We have to or where are we gonna end up?

Eleven – This Afternoon

Greta   Greta Stone and Thea Jones – we rhyme, maybe we fit together just like a jigsaw.

Thea   I'm very much an island, love – craggy edges to keep people away, many boats have cracked on these rocks. When you've spent your life losing people you have to protect yourself.

Greta (takes out the photo)   Is that someone you've lost?

Thea   How the hell did you get that? (**Snatches the photo.**) Give me that back.

Greta   But who is that?

Thea   Don't go poking about in my things.

Greta   I want to know about people.

Thea   Well, people might not want you to know.

What else have you got in your pocket?

Greta   Nothing, I promise.

Thea   Or in your bag – give it to me (**Thea taking things out of Greta's bag over next few lines.**)

Greta   I wouldn't do that.

Thea   Shush, it is not your turn to speak. I knew you were going to be trouble, I let you go into my office to charge your phone and this is what you do.

Greta   I just wanted to know about the man and the baby.

Thea   It's not all about you, Greta.

Greta   There's just things I need to know.

Thea   It's none of your business. Some things are too painful to talk about, especially to strangers. (**Realises there's nothing else in Greta's bag.**)

Greta   Oh. I hadn't thought of that. I thought you'd be happy to tell me about him. (**Picks up the photograph.**)

Thea   You haven't given a second thought to me here and now you're trying to steal things. (**Snatches the photograph back.**)

Greta   I thought it was important to talk to you, that's all.

Thea   You really are a selfish ticket.

Greta   No, I mean I came here to talk to you. To Northvale. I found out you were here and I want to know who I am. (**Takes a folded piece of paper from her pocket.**)

Thea   Something else you've taken without asking.

Greta   I wanted to see you and to talk to you. I know who you are, you see.

Thea   What are you going on about?

Greta   I changed my name to Greta Stone which is why I am so proud of saying it. And now I am Greta Stone.

Thea   I know, I know, you tell us often enough.

Greta   But I think that might be me in the photo. I used to be called Teagan Jones. That's the name my family gave me.

Thea (is shocked, upset)   Is this some kind of joke? You've told me that you are Greta Stone so many times.

Greta   But I was Teagan Jones. And that's me, isn't it? With my dad. Your big brother, Tony Jones. And you are Thea Jones.

Thea (looks at her face)   Teagan? (**Confused.**) You shouldn't have come here. I'm not here to be found like this. Why didn't you say when you first got here – you have totally messed me around.

Greta   I wanted to see you first. To hear you. I wanted to know if you did have a heart of gold.

Thea   Oh don't tell me the results of your findings on that please.

Greta   Aren't you excited to meet me? I wanted to know if I would recognise you but I didn't. And I don't recognise my dad either but I saw the photo and knew it must be him, must be us.

Thea   Tony died, you know that do you?

Greta   Yes, Jan told me that. First my mother died when I was a baby and then my dad died when I wasn't here.

Thea   Well that's where the trail ends, love, whoever you are. Now, if you'll just let me go and do my jobs.

Greta   Didn't you want me?

Thea   I don't know what you want to hear but you're not going to make me feel bad. We spent a lifetime looking after Tony, the alcohol, not knowing if he was going to live or die. A child would have just made it worse. And it would have been no life for a child.

Greta   But he could have lived for me.

Thea   But he just couldn't. He didn't expect to lose Jeannie. He could barely go on. And I don't want to talk about this anymore.

Greta   Did he blame me? Did he blame me for Jeannie's death?

Thea does not reply.

Greta   He did then, he did blame me.

Thea   He just saw you and felt the loss of her.

Twelve – Mid-afternoon Today

Greta

    I decide not to run, agree to see her.
    Thea lets us use her office. Official business.
    Jan seems different.
    The lapels on her jacket are sharper
    Her clipboard is new and shiny
    I can see my reflection
    On the back of it, distorted.
    Her smile is forced – it doesn't go right to the edges.

People think people like me don't read faces, but some of us do. We know when you're sincere and when you're not.

Jan with clipboard in hand, sits and Greta is standing.

Jan   Come and sit down, Greta, you'll be more comfortable.

Greta   I want to stand.

Jan   Contrary as ever, suit yourself. As you know I'm here to chat about what's going on at the moment. You are disappointed about the flat but this isn't the most mature way to approach it.

Greta   I didn't know what else to do.

Jan   What were you trying to achieve, coming here and bothering strangers.

Greta   I wasn't bothering people. I want to find my family.

Jan   Well, we've always done our best for you at the Magpie's Nest and you've repaid us with all this worry and all this extra paperwork. This wasn't in the plan, Greta.

Greta   Which plan, my care plan, my housing plan, my exiting care plan, my learning social cues plan, lots of plans that I didn't have a say in, lots of pieces of paper, locked in a filing cabinet in an office in our home that I have no access to.

Jan   Lots of people are working very hard so that you can have a smooth transition.

Greta   Most of them I've never met.

Jan   That's just how the system works.

Greta   Or doesn't work – the flat fell through, remember. I never got adopted. Do you remember telling me to smile?

Jan   What?

Greta   Every Friday afternoon, when the families were coming looking for someone to adopt or foster. You never thought I stood a chance, but you told me to smile anyway.

Jan   I'm not here to rake over the past. I have a questionnaire to go through with you, let's get through this and get you back to the Magpie.

Greta   The Magpie is not my home.

Jan   Let's remind ourselves of what you are good at and what you find difficult shall we, Greta?

Let's think about how you talk and interact.

Greta doesn't answer.

Jan   You struggle to get on with other people. We don't want people to think you are rude, do we? I know you want to fit in. Am I making sense Greta?

What about your routines, and all the noise - you must have found all this overwhelming.

Did you even bring a toothbrush? Our personal care is very important isn't it?

We understand that you really want to find your family but it's official business. You can't just turn up out of the blue. You have to do it right. You don't' know what they've got going on in their own lives. And they did made some decisions in the past didn't they and we should respect that. Am I making sense?

Greta   Those notes on the file I don't get to see. Damage – me and Kia once put passport photos of all us kids on the Welcome Wall. It was all photos of the staff and not one photograph of any of us anywhere in that home.

Jan   The Blu Tack left oily marks on the wall.

Greta   And you were going to make me and Kia pay for it to be repainted.

Jan   And shouting in public places.

Greta   Once that happened, at the cinema and it was hilarious. Believe me, I've wanted to shout on many more occasions than that.

Jan   Well there you go, you're making my case for me.

Greta

      My words don't fit their jigsaw.
      I tell them about the bricks and blocks
      That have been put in my way.

It's okay to take them down,
One at a time
But you can't squash me to fit,
the world needs to change its shape a bit
for people like me.
I have no real say,
you hold all the cards in your hands.
My card is pretty useless now.
You just talk about what's wrong with me and not what's right
You talk about what's wrong with me and not what's right
You talk about what's wrong with me and not what's right.

Thea   Okay, I've heard enough this is bullshit.

Greta   Thea comes in and puts her hand on my shoulder.

Thea   This is Greta Stone and she is twenty-one years old and she has nothing wrong with her. You have not been listening to her. She deserves more than this. Am I making any sense, Jan? She is staying here with us, if she wants to. Would you like to stay for a while Greta? I might not have the heart of gold you were looking for but I know what's right. I do. I know what's right. She is my niece and she will be staying here for a while She is twenty-one years old and she is a woman.

Greta   And she answered all their questions, signed something they showed her and she has to go to a meeting with me and they have agreed to a trial period and I can stay here.

I shimmy up the lamppost, it's all so easy now
A helium balloon from a party I never had
has lifted me up, allowed me to get to the top
and I take my time, think carefully
the art of persuasion is always on my mind
The city, the country, life all around me
And I can see everything from here.

Thirteen – Tonight

Thea is on stage at the microphone addressing the fundraiser audience.

Thea

> Tomorrow the doors open
> renewed purpose and
> new people.
> Sitting bravely here
> In the shadow of that steeple
> The council couldn't give a shit
> So communities have to do our bit
> Communities have to do our bit.

So, as we know, tomorrow the food bank goes full time and this very room will become our new community café serving free hot food to those that need it. And you lot are our little guinea pigs, but as Boris said many a time during the pandemic, 'make no mistake this is not a party'. It's not though, it's not a celebration, cos it's a bloody disgrace that we need to be doing this. I want to commend this community for pulling together, people from all parts of our communities have made donations, so you lovely lot, get your raffle tickets. We'll draw it at the break, Big Garry, when we'll also be serving – by popular demand – my famous piping hot, completely free, Love Soup. And those little cards on the table for your comments – keep it clean please, I do not need to know if you think I've got a big fat arse thank you very much Johnny Stanger – they're for offers of help. We want to know what you're going to do about all this. **(Gets busy setting tables etc.)**

Greta (wiping soup bowls with a tea towel)   Kia is coming tonight. I can't wait to see her. She is bringing her foster mum. Thea has offered me a volunteer role for the café – a try out to see if I like it. **(Whispers conspiratorially.)** I love it. I have never had a job before.

The busy-ness of the fundraiser starts again.

Greta   And already I have had some good ideas. Thea says so. I am concerned about disabled people who cannot get out of their houses, being unable to get to food banks and community cafés, and so we have to think about how to include everyone in the community. Thea says, 'When a society is on its knees is a test of its humanity and a real test of community'. If we did things in the pandemic when it suited everyone, we can do them now for people who are having care package cuts, reduced benefits, being sanctioned, people who need Love Soup the most. This isn't about feeling sorry for people, this is about how societies are organised, it's about solidarity and community. Save your tears, your pity is an indulgence I cannot afford. Turn tears into action. Do things. Make things happen.

Fourteen – Now

Audience song sheets, blankets, love soup.

Thea gives her a song sheet. Greta joins in with the song quietly at first. Thea joins after a few lines.

<Hunger No More>

Thea

Hold me
In the long nights
When we awaken
Let it be together
Eyes open wide
Forever
What are we waiting for
What should we be fighting for
Let Us All Be Counted
Hunger No More
Hunger No More
Full bellies and full minds
Now is the time
Raise up our voices, together
Speak all the words we held back
All the hungry years
When you look back in history
Lean faces came together
And walked the length of this country
Loud were the chants
that echo now through history

Let Us All Be Counted
Hunger No more
Hunger No more
Feed the people children first
Hunger no more
'Cause there is nothing worse
Than a stomach howling in pain
Take action now
Walk the streets of this country again
Let our voices come together
Hunger no more
Inequality no more
While leaders feast and drink
And turn their eyes away
with no humanity
we serve love soup
Silence no more
hunger no more
hunger no more
hunger no more
hunger no more